Intercessory

Prayer

HARVESTIME INTERNATIONAL INSTITUTE

This course is part of the **Harvestime International Institute**, a program designed to equip believers for effective spiritual harvest.

The basic theme of the training is to teach what Jesus taught, that which took men who were fishermen, tax collectors, etc., and changed them into reproductive Christians who reached their world with the Gospel in a demonstration of power.

This manual is a single course in one of several modules of curriculum which moves believers from visualizing through deputizing, multiplying, organizing, and mobilizing to achieve the goal of evangelizing.

TABLE OF CONTENTS

HOW TO USE THIS MANUAL

MANUAL FORMAT

Each lesson consists of:

Objectives: These are the goals you should achieve by studying the chapter. Read them before starting the lesson.

Key Verse: This verse emphasizes the main concept of the chapter. Memorize it.

Chapter Content: Study each section. Use your Bible to look up any references not printed in the manual.

Self-Test: Take this test after you finish studying the chapter. Try to answer the questions without using your Bible or this manual. When you have concluded the Self-Test, check your answers in the answer section provided at the end of the book.

For Further Study: This section will help you continue your study of the Word of God, improve your study skills, and apply what you have learned to your life and ministry.

Final Examination: If you are enrolled in this course for credit, you received a final examination along with this course. Upon conclusion of this course, you should complete this examination and return it for grading as instructed.

ADDITIONAL MATERIALS NEEDED

You will need a King James version of the Bible.

SUGGESTIONS FOR GROUP STUDY

FIRST MEETING

Opening: Open with prayer and introductions. Get acquainted and register the students.

Establish Group Procedures: Determine who will lead the meetings, the time, place, and dates for the sessions.

Praise And Worship: Invite the presence of the Holy Spirit into your training session.

Distribute Manuals To Students: Introduce the manual title, format, and course objectives provided in the first few pages of the manual.

Make The First Assignment: Students will read the chapters assigned and take the Self-Tests prior to the next meeting.   The number of chapters you cover per meeting will depend on chapter length, content, and the abilities of your group.

SECOND AND FOLLOWING MEETINGS

Opening: Pray. Welcome and register any new students and give them a manual. Take attendance. Have a time of praise and worship.

Review: Present a brief summary of what you studied at the last meeting.

Lesson: Discuss each section of the chapter using the **HEADINGS IN CAPITAL BOLD FACED LETTERS** as a teaching outline. Ask students for questions or comments on what they have studied. Apply the lesson to the lives and ministries of your students.

Self-Test: Review the Self-Tests students have completed.   (Note: If you do not want the students to have access to the answers to the Self-Tests, you may remove the answer pages from the back of each manual.)

For Further Study: You may do these projects on a group or individual basis.

Final Examination: If your group is enrolled in this course for credit, you received a final examination with this course. Reproduce a copy for each student and administer the exam upon conclusion of this course.

INTRODUCTION

You are about to begin an exciting spiritual adventure. Through the pages of this manual you will learn about a powerful supernatural resource available to the Body of Christ, that of intercessory prayer.

In this study you will learn what intercessory prayer is and how to do it effectively using dynamic spiritual resources that have been delegated for this purpose. You will learn what to pray for, how to overcome hindrances to intercessory prayer, and how to get started and keep going.

Your spiritual life and ministry will never again be the same. Are you ready to begin your journey to this exciting spiritual destination?

> There is a place where thou canst touch the eyes
> Of blinded men to instant perfect sight;
> There is a place where thou canst say, "Arise!"
> To dying captives, bound in chains of night.
>
> There is a place where thou cast reach the store
> Of hoarded gold and free it for the Lord;
> There is a place upon some distant shore
> Where thou canst send the worker and the Word;
> There is a place where heaven's resistant power
> Responsive moves to thine insistent plea;
>
> There is a place-a silent trysting hour-
> Where God Himself descends and fights for thee.
> Where is that secret place?   Dost thou ask where?
> O soul, it is the secret place of prayer!

-Author Unknown

COURSE OBJECTIVES

Upon conclusion of this course you will be able to:

- Define prayer.
- Explain how prayer is answered.
- Summarize the role of prayer in the life of Jesus Christ.
- Identify the levels of prayer.
- Identify the different types of prayer.
- Define intercessory prayer.
- Explain the Biblical basis of the believer's ministry as an intercessor.
- Identify Jesus Christ as our model for intercession.
- Describe how intercession is done.
- Explain why intercession is important.
- Use spiritual resources for intercession, including delegated power and authority, binding and loosing, the Name of Jesus, the blood of Jesus, and fasting.
- Explain how to intercede.
- Summarize principles for effective intercession.
- Identify what to intercede for.
- Use the promises of God to intercede.
- Identify and eliminate hindrances to effective intercession.
- Know when not to pray.
- Provide Scriptural references for the model prayer.
- Explain why the Lord's prayer is actually a prayer of intercession.
- Recite the model prayer from memory.
- Use the model prayer as a guide for intercession.
- Define revival.
- Explain how we can prepare for revival.
- Recognize when revival is needed.
- Identify evidences of a backslidden condition.
- Summarize Biblical principles of revival.
- Identify obstacles to revival.
- Explain how to use "God's revival plan" to intercede for revival.
- Make a plan for organized prayer.
- Create a personal prayer manual.
- Engage in international intercession.
- Identify problems and solutions for getting started and keeping going.
- Commit yourself to the ministry of intercession.

CHAPTER ONE

AN INTRODUCTION TO PRAYER

OBJECTIVES:

Upon completion of this chapter you will be able to:

- Define prayer.
- Explain how prayer is answered.
- Summarize the role of prayer in the life of Jesus Christ.
- Identify the levels of prayer.
- Identify the different types of prayer.

KEY VERSES:

> **Ask, and it shall be given you; seek, and ye shall find; knock, and it shall be opened unto you:**
>
> **For every one that asketh receiveth; and he that seeketh findeth, and to him that knocketh it shall be opened.   (Matthew 7:7-8)**

INTRODUCTION

This chapter introduces the subject of prayer. You will learn the definition of prayer and the importance Jesus placed on it. You will learn how prayer is answered and the different levels and types of prayer.

THE DEFINITION OF PRAYER

Prayer is communicating with God. It takes different forms, but basically it occurs when man talks with God and God talks with man. Prayer is described as:

Calling upon the name of the Lord:	Genesis 12:8
Crying unto God:	Psalms 27:7; 34:6
Drawing near to God:	Psalms 73:28; Hebrews 10:22
Looking up:	Psalms 5:3
Lifting up the soul:	Psalms 25:1
Lifting up the heart:	Lamentations 3:41
Pouring out the heart:	Psalms 62:8
Pouring out the soul:	I Samuel 1:15
Crying to Heaven:	II Chronicles 32:20
Beseeching the Lord:	Exodus 32:11

Seeking God:	Job 8:5
Seeking the face of the Lord:	Psalms 27:8
Making supplication:	Job 8:5; Jeremiah 36:7

Prayer is not just talking to God, but it involves listening also. Prayer is communication, and a one-way conversation does not last long. When you pray, expect God to speak to you. Most often He will do this through His written Word or by a "still small voice" that seems to "speak" to your heart. Sometimes He will give you a vision or interpret back to your spirit what you have prayed in your heavenly prayer language.

Don't just rush in and dump all your requests on God and then end your prayer. Allow time for Him to speak to you. He will give answers to your questions, guidance for the day ahead, and help you order your priorities. Sometimes He will give you a special message of encouragement to share with someone for whom you are interceding.

When you pray, there is no one approved posture for prayer. You may pray while:

Standing:	I Kings 8:22; Mark 11:25
Bowing down:	Psalms 95:6
Kneeling:	II Chronicles 6:13; Psalms 95:6; Luke 22:41; Acts 20:36
Falling on your face:	Numbers 16:22; Joshua 5:14; I Chronicles 21:16; Matthew 26:39
Spreading out your hands:	Isaiah 1:15; II Chronicles 6:13
Lifting up the hands:	Psalms 28:2; Lamentations 2:19; I Timothy 2:8

HOW PRAYER IS ANSWERED

The Bible reveals that prayer is answered:

Immediately at times:	Isaiah 65:24; Daniel 9:21-23
Delayed at times:	Luke 18:7
Different from our desires:	II Corinthians 12:8-9
Beyond our expectations:	Jeremiah 33:3; Ephesians 3:20

THE PRAYER LIFE OF JESUS

Prayer should be important to us because it was important to the Lord Jesus. Jesus is our greatest model of intercessory prayer. Study each of the following references about the prayer life of Jesus:

JESUS MADE PRAYER A PRIORITY:

-He prayed any time of the day or night:	Luke 6:12-13
-Prayer took priority over eating:	John 4:31-32
-Prayer took priority over business:	John 4:31-32
-He taught prayer to his disciples:	Matthew 6:9-13

PRAYER ACCOMPANIED ANY EVENT OF IMPORTANCE IN HIS LIFE:

-At His baptism:	Luke 3:21-22
-During the first ministry tour:	Mark 1:35; Luke 5:16
-Before the choice of the disciples:	Luke 6:12-13
-Before/after feeding the 5,000:	Matthew 14:19,23; Mark 6:41,46; John 6:11,14-15
-At the feeding of the 4,000:	Matthew 15:36; Mark 8:6,7
-Before the confession of Peter:	Luke 9:20
-Before the transfiguration:	Luke 9:28,29
-At the return of the seventy:	Matthew 11:25; Luke 10:21
-At the grave of Lazarus:	John 11:41-42
-At the blessing of the children:	Matthew 19:13
-At the coming of certain Greeks:	John 12:27-28
-For Peter:	Luke 22:32
-For the giving of the Holy Spirit:	John 14:16
-On the road to Emmaus:	Luke 24:30-31
-Prior to His ascension:	Luke 24:50-53
-For His followers:	John 17
-Before His greatest trial:	Matthew 26:26-27; Mark 14:22-23; Luke 22:17-19

LEVELS OF PRAYER

There are three levels of intensity in prayer: Asking, seeking, and knocking:

Ask, and it shall be given you; seek, and ye shall find; knock, and it shall be opened unto you:

For every one that asketh receiveth; and he that seeketh findeth, and to him that knocketh it shall be opened.   (Matthew 7:7-8)

Asking is the first level of prayer.   It is simply presenting a request to God and receiving an immediate answer.   In order to receive, the condition is to ask:

...ye have not, because ye ask not.   (James 4:2)

Seeking is a deeper level of prayer. This is the level of prayer where answers are not as immediate as at the asking level. The 120 gathered in the upper room where they continued in prayer is an example of seeking. These men and women sought fulfillment of the promise of the Holy Spirit and continued seeking until the answer came (Acts 1-2).

Knocking is a deeper level. It is prayer that is persistent when answers are longer in coming. It is illustrated by the parable Jesus told in Luke 11:5-10. It is also illustrated by the persistence of Daniel who continued to "knock" despite the fact he saw no visible results because Satan hindered the answer from God (Daniel 10).

TYPES OF PRAYER

Paul calls for believers to pray always with "all prayer" (Ephesians 6:18).   Another translation of the Bible reads "praying with every kind of prayer" (Goodspeed Translation). This refers to the various types of prayer which include:

1. WORSHIP AND PRAISE:

You enter into God's presence with worship and praise:

> **Enter into His gates with thanksgiving, and into His courts with praise; be thankful unto Him, and bless His Name.   (Psalms 100:4)**

Worship is the giving of honor and devotion.   Praise is thanksgiving and an expression of gratitude not only for what God has done but for who He is.   You are to worship God in spirit and in truth:

> **But the hour cometh, and now is, when the true worshipers shall worship the Father in Spirit and in truth: for the Father seeketh such to worship Him.**
>
> **God is a Spirit, and they that worship Him must worship Him in spirit and in truth.   (John 4:23-24)**

Worshiping God in truth means that you worship Him on the basis of what is revealed in the Word of God.   To worship Him in Spirit is to do so sincerely in the power of the Holy Spirit, from your innermost being, putting Him first above all others. When you worship in Spirit, you allow the Holy Spirit to direct your worship. You do not use man-made formulas or rituals of worship.   You do not just repeat chants or prayers with your mind somewhere else.

Instead, you open up the innermost recesses of your heart and mind, and lift praise and adoration to Him in your own words.   Sometimes, the Holy Spirit will take over completely and you will begin to worship in the "other tongues" of your prayer language.

Praise and worship can be with:

Singing:	Psalms 9:2,11; 40:3; Mark 14:26
Audible praise:	Psalms 103:1
Shouting:	Psalms 47:1
Lifting up of the hands:	Psalms 63:4; 134:2; I Timothy 2:8
Clapping:	Psalms 47:1
Musical instruments:	Psalms 150:3-5
Standing:	II Chronicles 20:19
Bowing:	Psalms 95:6
Dancing:	Psalms 149:3
Kneeling:	Psalms 95:6
Lying down:	Psalms 149:5

2. COMMITMENT:

This is prayer committing your life and will to God.   It includes prayers of consecration and dedication to God, His work, and His purposes.

3. PETITION:

Prayers of petition are requests.   Requests must be made according to the will of God as revealed in His written Word.   Petitions may be at the levels of asking, seeking, or knocking. Supplication is another word for this type of prayer.   The word supplication means "beseeching God or strongly appealing to Him in behalf of a need.

4. CONFESSION AND REPENTANCE:

A prayer of confession is repenting and asking forgiveness for sin:

> **If we confess our sins, He is faithful and just to forgive us our sins and to cleanse us from all unrighteousness. (I John 1:9)**

5. INTERCESSION:

Intercession is prayer for others.   An intercessor is one who takes the place of another or pleads another's case.   It is upon this type of prayer that the remainder of this manual focuses.

SELF-TEST

1.   Write the Key Verse from memory.

____

____

2.   Define prayer.

____

____

3.   Explain how prayer is answered.

____

____

4.   Summarize the role of prayer in the life of Jesus Christ.

____

____

5.   Identify and define the levels of prayer discussed in this chapter.

____

6.   Write a brief synopsis of the five types of prayer discussed in this chapter.

____

____

____

(Answers to tests are provided at the conclusion of the final chapter in this manual.)

FOR FURTHER STUDY

1. Here is a prayer guide to help you pray for the continents and the world:

    On Monday: Pray for Asia
    On Tuesday: Pray for Europe
    On Wednesday: Pray for Africa
    On Thursday: Pray for North America
    On Friday: Pray for Latin America
    On Saturday: Pray for Oceania (Island nations)
    On Sunday: Pray for the entire world

2. Study the following Scriptures again and then experiment by praying in different positions:

    Standing: I Kings 8:22; Mark 11:25
    Bowing down: Psalms 95:6
    Kneeling: II Chronicles 6:13; Psalms 95:6; Luke 22:41; Acts 20:36
    Falling on your face: Numbers 16:22; Joshua 5:14; I Chronicles 21:16; Matthew 26:39
    Spreading out your hands: Isaiah 1:15; II Chronicles 6:13
    Lifting up the hands: Psalms 28:2; Lamentations 2:19; I Timothy 2:8

3. Study the following verses again and then experiment by praising and worshiping God in the various ways Scripture directs:

    Singing: Psalms 9:2,11; 40:3; Mark 14:26
    Audible praise: Psalms 103:1
    Shouting: Psalms 47:1
    Lifting up of the hands: Psalms 63:4; 134:2; I Timothy 2:8
    Clapping: Psalms 47:1
    Musical instruments: Psalms 150:3-5
    Standing: II Chronicles 20:19
    Bowing: Psalms 95:6
    Dancing: Psalms 149:3
    Kneeling: Psalms 95:6
    Lying down: Psalms 149:5

CHAPTER TWO
INTERCESSORY PRAYER

OBJECTIVES:

Upon completion of this chapter you will be able to:

- Define intercessory prayer.
- Explain the Biblical basis of the believer's ministry as an intercessor.
- Identify Jesus Christ as our model for intercession.
- Explain how to intercede.
- Explain why intercession is important.

KEY VERSE:

> **Wherefore He is able also to save them to the uttermost that come unto God
> by Him, seeing He ever liveth to make intercession for them.**
> **(Hebrews 7:25)**

INTRODUCTION

In the last lesson you learned that **intercession** is praying for others. An **intercessor** is one who takes the place of another or pleads another's case.   When you pray this way, you are **interceding**:

> *"Intercession may be defined as holy, believing, persevering prayer whereby
> someone pleads with God on behalf of another or others who desperately need
> God's intervention."   (Full Life Bible)*

It is upon this type of prayer that the remainder of this manual focuses.   In this lesson you will learn the Biblical basis of intercession and about our model for intercession, the Lord Jesus Christ.   You will also learn how to do intercession and why it is an important ministry.

THE BIBLICAL BASIS OF INTERCESSION

The Biblical basis for the New Testament believer's ministry of intercessory prayer is our calling as priests unto God.   The Word of God declares that we are a holy priesthood (I Peter 2:5), a royal priesthood (I Peter 2:9), and a kingdom of priests (Revelation 1:5).

The background for understanding this calling to priestly intercession is found in the Old Testament example of the Levitical priesthood.   The priest's responsibility was to stand **before** and **between**.   He stood before God to minister to Him with sacrifices and offerings.   The priests also stood between a righteous God and sinful man bringing them together at the place of the blood sacrifice.

Hebrews 7:11-19 explains the difference between the Old and New Testament ministries of the priest.   The Old Testament Levitical priesthood was passed on from generation to generation through the descendants of the tribe of Levi.   "The Melchizedek priesthood" spoken of in this passage, is the "new order" of spiritual priests of whom the Lord Jesus is the High Priest. It is passed on to us through His blood and our spiritual birth as new creatures in Christ.

THE MODEL INTERCESSOR

The Bible records that God's purpose in sending Jesus was for Him to serve as an intercessor:

> **And He saw that there was no man, and wondered that there was no intercessor: therefore His arm brought salvation unto Him, and His righteousness, it sustained Him.   (Isaiah 59:16)**

Jesus stands before God and between Him and sinful man, just as the Old Testament priests did:

> **For there is one God, and one mediator (intercessor) between God and men, the man Christ Jesus.   (I Timothy 2:5)**

> **...It is Christ that died, yea rather, that is risen again, who is even at the right hand of God, who also maketh intercession for us.   (Romans 8:34)**

> **Wherefore He is able also to save them to the uttermost that come unto God by Him, seeing He ever liveth to make intercession for them. (Hebrews 7:25)**

Jesus brings sinful man and a righteous God together at the place of the blood sacrifice for sin. No longer is the blood of animals necessary as it was in the Old Testament. We can now approach God on the basis of the blood of Jesus which was shed on the cross of Calvary for the remission of sins. Because of the blood of Jesus, you can approach God boldly without timidity (Hebrews 4:14-16).

Jesus was an intercessor while He was here on earth. He prayed for those who were sick and possessed by demons. He prayed for His disciples. He even prayed for you when He interceded for all those who would believe on Him. Jesus continued His ministry of intercession after His death and resurrection when He returned to Heaven. He now serves as our intercessor in Heaven.

HOW TO INTERCEDE

As intercessors following the Old Testament priestly function and the New Testament pattern of Jesus, we stand before God and between a righteous God and sinful man. In order to be effective standing "between" we must first stand "before" God to develop the intimacy necessary to fulfill this role.

Numbers 14 is one of the greatest accounts of intercessory prayer recorded in the Bible. Moses was able to stand between God and sinful man because he had stood "before" Him and had developed intimacy. Numbers 12:8 records that God spoke with Moses as friend to friend and not through visions and dreams as He did with other prophets.

As New Testament believers we no longer sacrifice animals as in Old Testament times. We stand before the Lord to offer up spiritual sacrifices of praise (Hebrews 13:5) and the sacrifice of our own lives (Romans 12:1). It is on the basis of this intimate relationship with God that we can then stand "between" Him and others, serving as an advocate and intercessor in their behalf.

Peter uses two words to describe this priestly ministry: "Holy" and "royal." Holiness is required to stand before the Lord (Hebrews 12:14). We are able to do it only on the basis of the righteousness of Christ not our own righteousness. Royalty is descriptive of the kingly authority which is delegated to us as members of the "royal family," so to speak, with legitimate access to the throne room of God.

Sometimes this priestly intercession is done with understanding.   This occurs when you intercede for others in your own native language and you understand what you are saying:

> **I exhort therefore, that first of   all, supplications, prayers, intercessions, and giving of thanks, be made for all men.**
>
> **For kings, and for all that are in authority... (I Timothy 2:1-2)**

At other times, intercession is made by the Holy Spirit.   It may be with groanings resulting from a heavy spiritual burden. It may also be in an unknown tongue. When this happens, the Holy Spirit speaks through you praying directly to God according to the will of God:

> **Likewise the Spirit also helpeth our infirmities; for we know not what we should pray for as we ought; but the Spirit itself maketh intercession for us with groanings which cannot be uttered.   (Romans 8:26)**
>
> **For he who speaks in a tongue does not speak to men but to God, for no one understands him; however, in the spirit he speaks mysteries. (I Corinthians 14:2)**

You do not understand this type of intercession with your mind, but it is the deepest level of intercessory prayer and the most effective because it is made "according to the will of God." Your mind and will do not affect the prayers prayed by the Holy Spirit through you in an unknown tongue.[1]

WHY INTERCESSION IS IMPORTANT

Intercession is obviously important because of the emphasis Jesus placed on it in His own earthly ministry. Its importance is also revealed in the Biblical record which is filled with the stories of men and women who experienced powerful results through effective intercession.

Through effective intercession, you can go spiritually anywhere in the world. Your prayers have no limitations of distance as they can penetrate unreached nations and cross through geographical, cultural, and political barriers. You can affect the destiny of individuals and entire nations. You can actually help save lives and souls of men and women, boys and girls and extend the Gospel of the Kingdom of God around the world as you intercede in prayer.

---

[1]   For additional information on speaking in other tongues consult the Harvestime International Institute course entitled *"Ministry Of The Holy Spirit."*

SELF-TEST

1.   Write the Key Verse from memory.

____

____

2.   Define intercessory prayer.

____

____

3.   Explain the Biblical basis of the believer's ministry as an intercessor.

____

____

____

4.   Who is our model for intercession?

____

5.   Explain how intercession is done.

____

____

6.   Explain why intercession is important.

____

____

(Answers to tests are provided at the conclusion of the final chapter in this manual.)

FOR FURTHER STUDY

One of the greatest examples of intercessory prayer is the prayer of Jesus recorded in John 17. Use the following outline to study this prayer:

Jesus prays for Himself: **John 17:1-5**

Summarize His requests for Himself:

____

Jesus prays for His immediate disciples: **John 17:6-19**

Summarize His requests for His immediate disciples:

____

Jesus prays for His future disciples: **John 17:20-23**

List the specific requests Jesus makes for His future disciples:

____

Jesus concludes His prayer: **John 17:24-26**

Summarize how Jesus concludes His prayer:

____

What is His specific desire?

____

What did He declare to His followers?

____

What does He want to be "in them"?_______________________________

CHAPTER THREE

SPIRITUAL RESOURCES FOR INTERCESSION

OBJECTIVES:

Upon completion of this chapter you will be able to:

- Identify the spiritual resources for intercession, including:
- Delegated power and authority.
- Binding and loosing.
- The Name of Jesus.
- The Blood of Jesus.
- Fasting.
- Use these spiritual resources in intercession.

KEY VERSE:

> **Then He called His twelve disciples together and gave them power and authority over all devils, and to cure diseases. (Luke 9:1)**

INTRODUCTION

God has provided tremendous spiritual resources for this ministry of intercession to which we are called.   In this lesson you will learn how to use these resources which include delegated power and authority, binding and loosing, the Name of Jesus, the blood of Jesus and fasting.

DELEGATED POWER AND AUTHORITY

When we intercede in prayer we actually battle with our enemy, Satan,   for the souls of men and women, boys and girls, for nations, and spiritual and political leaders.   We do not do this in our own ability or strength, but on the basis of the spiritual power and authority delegated to us by Jesus:

> **Then He called His twelve disciples together and gave them power and authority over all devils, and to cure diseases. (Luke 9:1)**

There is a difference between authority and power. Consider the example of a policeman. He has a badge and a uniform which are symbols of his authority. His authority comes because of the position he holds with the government. Since not all people respect that authority, the policeman also carries a weapon and that weapon is his power. Your authority over the enemy comes through Jesus Christ and your position in Him as a believer. Your power over the enemy comes through the Holy Spirit:

> **And behold, I send the promise of My Father upon you; but tarry ye in the
> city of Jerusalem, until ye be endued with power from on high.**
> **(Luke 24:49)**

Like the policeman, you must have both authority and power to be effective in intercession, for you are actually doing spiritual battle with Satan. Believers receive authority through the new birth experience and their position in Christ but some never go on to receive the power of the Holy Spirit which must be combined with authority to intercede effectively.

Satan has limited power, but he has no authority.   Jesus gave us both power and authority over all the power of the enemy. The power Jesus gave is directed power to be used for specific purposes in intercession:

POWER OVER THE ENEMY:

You have authority to intercede in prayer for those who need healing and deliverance:

> **Then He called His twelve disciples together and gave them power and
> authority over all devils, and to cure diseases.   (Luke 9:1)**

POWER OVER SIN:

You have authority to intercede for those who need salvation:

> **Whosesoever sins ye remit, they are remitted unto them; and whosesoever
> sins ye retain, they are retained.   (John 20:23)**

POWER TO EXTEND THE GOSPEL:

You have authority to pray for laborers to extend the Gospel:

> **Then He said to His disciples, "The harvest truly is plentiful, but the laborers
> are few.   Therefore pray the Lord of the harvest to send out laborers into
> His harvest." (Matthew 9:37)**

BINDING AND LOOSING

The term "to bind" originates from the Hebrew word *asar* meaning "to bind, imprison, tie, gird, to harness."   The word occurs approximately 70 times in the Hebrew Old Testament and was often used to indicate the tying up of horses and donkeys (II Kings 7:10).

The remarks of Jesus in Matthew 12:28-29 are of great significance.

**But if I cast out demons by the Spirit of God, surely the kingdom of God has
come upon you.**

**Or else how can one enter a strong man's house and plunder his goods,
unless he first binds the strong man? And then he will plunder his house.
(Matthew 12:28-29)**

It is impossible to take the possessions of the strong man without first of all binding the strong
man. Jesus, in speaking of the strong man, is referring to Satan. Those possessions which are to
be taken from him are his most prized possessions of all, lost individuals enslaved by him,
including those who are "demonized."

Jesus gave believers the power to bind and loose:

**And I will give unto thee the keys of the Kingdom of Heaven; and whatsoever
thou shalt bind on earth shall be bound in Heaven; and whatsoever thou
shalt loose on earth shall be loosed in Heaven.
(Matthew 16:19)**

Jesus taught the importance of binding evil spirits before casting them out, but the principle of
binding and loosing extends to more than casting out demons. You can bind the power of the
enemy to work in your life, home, community, and church fellowship. You can loose men and
women from the bondage of sin, depression, and discouragement of the enemy.   In every
situation...every problem, every challenge...there is a spiritual key. That key is binding and
loosing through intercessory prayer.

THE NAME OF JESUS

The Name of Jesus is the authority upon which we intercede.   Jesus promised:
If ye shall ask any thing in my name, I will do it.   (John 14:14)

**...Verily, verily, I say unto you, Whatsoever ye shall ask the Father in my
name, He will give it you.   (John 16:23)**

**And these signs shall follow them that believe, IN MY NAME shall they cast
out devils; they shall speak with new tongues;**

**They shall take up serpents; and if they drink any deadly thing, it shall not
hurt them: they shall lay hands on the sick, and they shall recover.
(Mark 16:17-18)**

**And Jesus came and spake unto them, saying, All power is given unto me in
Heaven and in earth.**

Go ye therefore, and teach all nations, baptizing them in the name of the Father, and of the Son, and of the Holy Ghost;

Teaching them to observe all things, whatsoever I have commanded you; and, lo, I am with you alway, even unto the end of the world. (Matthew 28:18-20)

You are to pray, preach, teach, baptize, cast out demons, heal the sick, and overcome every power of the enemy through the name of Jesus. The name of Jesus is more powerful than any other name:

Far above all principality, and power, and might, and dominion, and every name that is named, not only in this world, but also in that which is to come. (Ephesians 1:21)

Wherefore God also hath highly exalted Him, and given Him a name which is above every name;

That at the name of Jesus every knee should bow, of things in Heaven, and things in earth, and things under the earth;

And that every tongue should confess that Jesus Christ is Lord, to the glory of God the Father.   (Philippians 2:9-11)

THE BLOOD OF JESUS

The blood of Jesus is another powerful spiritual resource that enables us to intercede.   It is through His blood that we have access to God the Father:

Therefore, brethren, having boldness to enter the Holiest by the blood of Jesus,

By a new and living way which He consecrated for us, through the veil, that is His flesh,

And having a High Priest over the house of God.

Let us draw near with a true heart in full assurance of faith, having our hearts sprinkled from an evil conscience and our bodies washed with pure water.

Let us hold fast the confession of our hope without wavering, for He who promised is faithful.   (Hebrews 10:19-23)

The "Holiest" is the place where God dwells.   We do not access God's presence by religious ritual or complicated procedures. We access it by the blood of Jesus Christ.

The subject of blood is a scarlet thread that runs throughout the entire Bible from Genesis to Revelation.   The Bible teaches that the life of man and beasts is in the blood (Leviticus 17:11,14). Because the penalty for sin is death (Romans 6:23) and since life is in the blood, God established the principle that forgiveness of sins comes only through the shedding of blood:

> **And according to the law almost all things are purged with blood, and without shedding of blood there is no remission (from sin).**
> **(Hebrews 9:22)**

God made the first blood sacrifice in the Garden of Eden after the sin of Adam and Eve when He killed animals and clothed the couple in skins which were representative of the righteousness of Christ.   The importance of the blood sacrifice is emphasized through the story of Cain and Abel, the covenant of circumcision with the Israelites and the Levitical ceremonies in the tabernacle. In the Old Testament the blood of animals was offered as sacrifice repeatedly whenever man sinned.   Hebrews 8 details this process and describes it as the "old covenant."

In the New Testament God sent Jesus to shed His blood for sin once and for all. His blood is described as the "new covenant" (Mark 14:24) and He is the mediator of this new covenant (Hebrews 8:6). This made the old covenant obsolete, meaning it is no longer necessary that the blood of animals be offered as a sacrifice for sin:

> **Not with the blood of goats and calves, but with His own blood He entered in the most holy place once for all, having obtained ETERNAL redemption. (Hebrews 9:12)**

Hebrews 12:24 indicates that the blood of Jesus speaks for us and what it confesses provides valuable eternal benefits for us. When Paul directs us to "hold fast our confession" (Hebrews 10:22), it relates back to the previous verses which indicates we have the right to draw near to the Holiest.

You enter God's presence in prayer the same way you are saved, by confessing the benefits of the blood of Jesus:

> **...If you confess with your mouth the Lord Jesus and believe in your heart that God has raised Him from the dead, you will be saved.**
>
> **For with the heart one believes to righteousness, and with the mouth confession is made to salvation.   (Romans 10:9-10)**

God acts in response to your confession which has authority because it is based on the testimony of the blood of Jesus. The blood declares that you can enter right now into the most holy place where God dwells and minister through intercession.

FASTING

Another spiritual resource for effective intercession is fasting. Fasting, in the most simple definition, is going without food. Fasting is one of the things that approves us as ministers of God (II Corinthians 6:3-10). Prayer with fasting was practiced in the early Church (Acts 14:23) and Paul encourages us to "give ourselves" to it (I Corinthians 7:5).

TYPES OF FASTS:

According to the Bible there are two types of fasts. The total fast is when you do not eat or drink at all. An example of this is found in Acts 9:9. The partial fast is when the diet is restricted. An example of this is in Daniel 10:3.

BIBLICAL EXAMPLES OF FASTING:

-Abraham's servant fasted while seeking the right bride for Isaac (Genesis 24:33).

-Moses fasted for 40 days and nights while receiving the revelations of the law and the tabernacle (Exodus 34).

-Hannah fasted for a child (11 Samuel 1:7-8).

-Nehemiah fasted for the restoration of Jerusalem (Nehemiah 1:4).

-The Jews fasted for deliverance following Haman's evil decree of death (Esther 4).

-The entire city of Ninevah fasted in response to Jonah's call for repentance (Jonah 3:5-10).

-David fasted just prior to assuming his God-given destiny as King of Israel (I Samuel 31).

-Daniel fasted for 21 days and at the conclusion received the message from God that launched the turning point for the Hebrews in captivity.

-Jehoshaphat proclaimed a fast prior to battle (2 Chronicles 20:3).

-Ezra called a fast of repentance for the exiles by the river Ahava (Ezra 8-9).

-Jesus fasted prior to entering His ministry (Matthew 4).

-The Apostle Paul fasted after his conversion (Acts 9).

21

-It was during a time of fasting that Peter received his commission to share the Gospel with the Gentiles and Cornelius was prepared to receive the revelation (Acts 10).

-The disciples were fasting and praying when the Holy Spirit separated Paul and Barnabas for missionary service (Acts 13:2).

THE PURPOSES OF FASTING:

Fasting does not change God. It changes you. God relates to you on the basis of your relationship to Him. When you change, then the way God deals with you is affected. You do not fast to change God because God does not change. Fasting does change how He deals with you. Read the book of Jonah for an example of this in the city of Ninevah.

On one occasion when the Disciples of Jesus failed to bring help to a demon possessed youngster, Jesus explained that "this kind" came out only by fasting and prayer (Mark 9:29). There are certain situations in life which you cannot face apart from prayer and fasting. More and more as the end time approaches, we will encounter "this kind" of situations, critical dilemmas we have never before experienced. Our victory over "this kind" will necessitate fasting.

There are definite spiritual purposes for fasting. It is important that you understand these purposes. If you fast for the wrong reasons or with no specific purpose, the fast will be ineffective. Study each of the following references. They reveal that people fasted:

-In response to a message from God:	Jonah 3:5
-During times of wilderness testing:	Luke 4:1
-During the threat of national calamity or war:	II Chronicles 20:3
-When revelation was needed from God:	Daniel 9:3-4
-When making decisions:	Acts 13:2-3
-When making special requests before authorities:	Esther 4:16
-To prepare for confrontation with demonic activity:	Mark 9:29
-To humble one's self:	Psalms 35:13; 69:10
-To repent of sin:	Joel 2:12
-To feed the poor, both physically and spiritually:	Isaiah 58:7
-To be heard of God:	II Samuel 12:16,22; Jonah 3:5,10
-To loose bands of wickedness, lift heavy burdens, set the oppressed free, and break every bondage:	Isaiah 58:6

LENGTH OF THE FAST:

How long you fast depends upon what God speaks into your spirit. He may lead you to fast a brief or lengthy time. Remember the story of Esau and Jacob? Jacob was originally making a meal for himself but denied himself in order to obtain the birthright. How much better if Esau had fasted that meal!

If you have never fasted begin by fasting one meal. Next you might want to try fasting from sundown one day to sundown the next night. Then you might increase your fasting to more lengthy periods of time. You should always drink water on long fasts. You can go without food for long periods, but water is needed to maintain bodily functions.

PUBLIC AND PRIVATE FASTING:

Fasting is a personal matter between an individual and God.   It is to be done in private and not boasted about:

> **Moreover when ye fast, be not as the hypocrites, of a sad countenance; for they disfigure their faces, that they may appear unto men to fast.   Verily I say unto you, they have their reward.**
>
> **But thou, when thou fastest, anoint thine head, and wash thy face;**
>
> **That thou appear not unto men to fast, but unto thy Father which is in secret and thy Father which seeth in secret shall reward thee openly.**
> **(Matthew 6:16-18)**

Leaders may call a public fast and request the whole church fellowship to fast:

> **Blow the trumpet in Zion, sanctify a fast, call a solemn assembly.**
> **(Joel 2:15)**

GOD'S CHOSEN FAST:

Isaiah 58 describes God's "chosen" or divinely approved fast. God's chosen fast is one:

> -Where you humble yourself before God: Verse 5
> -To loose the bonds of wickedness: Verse 6
> -Which undoes heavy burdens: Verse 6
> -That frees the oppressed: Verse 6
> -Done with unselfish motives and manifested charity: Verse 7

THE RESULTS OF FASTING:

When you fast, the first thing that happens is that God begins to reveal Himself to you.   The Father says, "Then you shall call, and the Lord will answer; You shall cry, and He will say, `Here am I'" (Isaiah 58:9).   Other results of fasting itemized in Isaiah 58 are:

-Illumination: Verses 8 and 10 declare that the dark periods of your life will become like noonday.   When others think they have extinguished your spiritual light, it will rise again and break forth like the morning.

-Direction: Verse 11 promises that   "the Lord will guide you continually."

-Provision: Verse 11 declares God will "satisfy your soul in drought."   (This can apply to both material and spiritually lean times.) Verse 11 also describes unlimited spiritual resources. You will be like a "well watered garden," and "a spring of water whose waters do not fail."

-Rejuvenation: Verse 11 declares God will "strengthen your bones" and verse 8 proclaims that "your healing shall spring forth speedily."

-Restoration: Verse 12 indicates that you and your spiritual seed "shall build the old waste places...raise up the foundations of many generations...And you shall be called the Repairer of the Breach, The Restorer of Streets to Dwell In."

RESOURCES FOR INTERCESSION

The believer has powerful spiritual resources to enable effective intercession.   As you have learned in this chapter, these include:

-Delegated power and authority.
-Binding and loosing.
-The Name of Jesus.
-The Blood of Jesus.
-Fasting.

SELF-TEST

1.   Write the Key Verse from memory.

____

____

2.   Explain the difference between spiritual power and authority.

____

____

3.   What does it mean to bind something spiritually?

____

____

4.   What does it mean to loose something spiritually?

____

____

5.   What Scripture gives us the authority to bind and loose?

____

6.   Explain why the name of Jesus is a powerful resource for intercession.

____

7.   Explain how the blood of Jesus is a resource for intercession.

____

8.   List and define the two types of Biblical fasts.

____

____

9.   Summarize the purposes for fasting.

____

____

10.   What Scriptural reference describes God's "chosen" fast?

____

11.   What are some of the positive results of fasting?

____

____

____

(Answers to tests are provided at the conclusion of the final chapter in this manual.)

FOR FURTHER STUDY

The Name of Jesus is the authority by which we intercede to God.   Study the following list of
His names to further your knowledge of the tremendous power inherent in the name of "Jesus":

Advocate	I John 2:1
Almighty	Revelation 1:8
Alpha and Omega	Revelation 21:6
Amen	Revelation 3:14
Author/Finisher of our Faith	Hebrews 12:2
Author of Eternal Salvation	Hebrews 5:9
Begotten of God	I John 5:18
Beloved	Ephesians 1:6
Branch	Zechariah 3:8
Bread of Life	John 6:48
Bright and Morning Star	Revelation 22:16
Captain of the Lord's Host	Joshua 5:15
Chief Cornerstone	I Peter 2:6
Chiefest Among Ten Thousand	Song of Solomon 5:10
Christ	John 1:41
Counselor	Isaiah 9:6
Deliverer	Romans 11:26
Door	John 10:9
Emmanuel	Matthew 1:23
Eternal Life	I John 5:20
Faithful and True	Revelation 19:11
Faithful Witness	Revelation 1:5
First Begotten	Hebrews 1:6
First and Last	Revelation 22:13
Glorious Lord	Isaiah 33:21
Great High Priest	Hebrews 4:14
Head of the Body	Colossians 1:18
Head over all things	Ephesians 1:22
Headstone	Psalms 118:22
Heir of all things	Hebrews 1:2
Holy One of Israel	Isaiah 41:14
Hope of Glory	Colossians 1:27
I Am	John 8:58
Image of the Invisible God	Colossians 1:15
Jesus Christ Our Lord	Romans 1:3
King of Glory	Psalms 24:7
Lamb of God	John 1:29
Light of the World	John 8:12
Lily of the Valleys	Song of Solomon 2:1

Living Bread	John 6:51
Lord God Almighty	Revelation 4:8
Lord of All	Acts 10:36
Lord Our Righteousness	Jeremiah 23:6
Love	1 John 4:8
Man of Sorrows	Isaiah 53:3
Master	Matthew 23:10
Messiah	Daniel 9:25
Most Holy	Daniel 9:24
Nazarene	Matthew 2:23
Only Wise God	I Timothy 1:17
Our Passover	I Corinthians 5:7
Physician	Luke 4:23
Prince of Peace	Isaiah 9:6
Propitiation	Romans 3:25
Redeemer	Isaiah 59:20
Resurrection	John 11:25
Righteous Servant	Isaiah 53:11
Rock	I Corinthians 10:4
Rose of Sharon	Song of Solomon 2:1
Savior of the World	I John 4:14
Shepherd	John 10:11
Son of God	Romans 1:4
Son of Man	Acts 7:56
Son of Mary	Mark 6:3
Stone	Matthew 21:42
Sure Foundation	Isaiah 28:16
Teacher	John 3:2
Truth	John 14:6
Unspeakable Gift	II Corinthians 9:15
Vine	John 15:1
Way	John 14:6
Wonderful	Isaiah 9:6
Word of God	Revelation 19:13

CHAPTER FOUR

HOW TO INTERCEDE

OBJECTIVES:

Upon completion of this chapter you will be able to:

- Explain how to intercede.
- Summarize principles for effective intercession.
- Identify what to intercede for.
- Use the promises of God to intercede.

KEY VERSES:

> **This is the confidence we have in approaching God; that if we ask anything according to His will, He hears us. And if we know that He hears us-whatever we ask-we know that we have what we asked of Him. (I John 5:14-15)**

INTRODUCTION

The key element in intercessory prayer is not how loud we pray, nor how energetic we are in our prayers (this is not say that these are wrong), but how sincere our requests are as we make them known unto God. It is imperative that God's glory be the end of our intercession because Satan's chief goal is to prevent God from being glorified. Therefore, if we are to have as our primary goal the glorification of God and commit our whole soul and being to the movement of intercessory prayer, God will manifest Himself. "Then you will call upon me and when you seek me with all your heart, I will be found by you..." (Jeremiah 29:12-13).

Prayer should be offered in faith and according to the will of God:

> **This is the confidence we have in approaching God; that if we ask anything according to His will, He hears us. And if we know that He hears us-whatever we ask-we know that we have what we asked of Him. (I John 5:14-15)**

In this lesson you will learn what the Bible teaches about how to intercede and what to intercede for. You will also learn how to base your intercession upon the promises of God's Word.

HOW TO INTERCEDE

Look up each of the following references in your Bible. These passages provide Biblical guidelines for intercession:

-Prayer is to be made to God:	Psalms 5:2
-Quality rather than quantity is stressed; Prayer is not successful because of "much speaking":	Matthew 6:7
-Empty repetition is forbidden, but earnest repetition is not:	Daniel 6:10; Luke 11:5-13; 18:1-8
-Pray with understanding (in a known tongue):	Ephesians 6:18
-Pray in the Spirit in tongues:	Romans 8:26; Jude 20
-Intercede according to the will of God:	I John 5:14-15
-Pray in secret:	Matthew 6:6
-Pray always:	Luke 21:36; Ephesians 6:18
-Pray continually without ceasing:	Romans 12:12; I Thessalonians 5:17
-Intercede to the Father in the name of Jesus:	John 14:13-14
-Pray with a watchful attitude:	I Peter 4:7
-Pray using the example of the model prayer:	Matthew 6:9-13
-Pray with a forgiving spirit:	Mark 11:25
-Pray with humility:	Matthew 6:7
-Sometimes accompany prayer with fasting:	Matthew 17:21
-Intercede fervently:	James 5:16; Colossians 4:12
-Pray with submission to God:	Luke 22:42
-Use the strategies of binding and loosing in prayer:	Matthew 16:19

PRINCIPLES FOR EFFECTIVE INTERCESSION

Here are some principles of effective intercession drawn from the foregoing Scriptures:

1. Praise God for who He is and for the privilege of engaging in the same wonderful ministry as the Lord Jesus (Hebrews 7:25). Praise God for the privilege of cooperating with Him in the affairs of men through prayer.

2. Make sure your heart is clean before God by having given the Holy Spirit time to convict, should there be any unconfessed sin (Psalms 66:28; 29:23-24).

3. Acknowledge you cannot really pray without the direction and energy of the Holy Spirit (Romans 8:26). Ask God to utterly control you by His Spirit, believe by faith that He does, and thank Him (Ephesians 5:18).

4. Deal aggressively with the enemy. Come against him in the all-powerful Name of the Lord Jesus Christ and with the "sword of the Spirit"--the Word of God (James 4:7).

5.   Die to your own imaginations, desires, and burdens for what you feel you should pray (Proverbs 3:5-6; 28:26; Isaiah 55:8).

6.   Praise God now in faith for the remarkable prayer meeting you are going to have.   He is a remarkable God and will do something consistent with His character.

7.   Wait before God in silent expectancy, listening for His direction (Psalms 62:5; Micah 7:7; Psalms 81:11-13).

8.   In obedience and faith, utter what God brings to your mind, believing (John 10:27). Keep asking God for direction, expecting Him to give it to you. He will (Psalms 32:8). Make sure you don't move to the next subject until you have given God time to discharge all He wants to say regarding this burden, especially when praying in a group. Be encouraged by the lives of Moses, Daniel, Paul, and Anna, knowing that God gives revelation to those who make intercession a way of life.

9.   If possible, have your Bible with you should God want to give you direction or confirmation from it (Psalms 119:10-15).

10.   When God ceases to bring things to your mind to pray for, finish by praising and thanking Him for what He has done, reminding yourself of Romans 11:36,"For from Him and through Him and to Him are all things. To Him be the glory forever! Amen." [1]

WHAT TO INTERCEDE FOR

Study the following Biblical references which reveal what you are to intercede for:

-The peace of Jerusalem:	Psalms 122:6
-Laborers in the harvest:	Matthew 9:38; Luke 10:2
-That you enter not into temptation:	Luke 22:40-46
-Them that despitefully use you (your enemies):	Luke 6:28
-All the saints:	Ephesians 6:18
-The sick:	James 5:14
-One for another (bearing others burdens):	James 5:16
(You sin by neglecting to pray for others:	I Samuel 12:23)
-For all men, kings, and those in authority:	I Timothy 2:1-4
-For daily needs:	Matthew 6:11
-For wisdom:	James 1:5
-For healing:	James 5:14-15
-For forgiveness:	Matthew 6:12
-For God's will and Kingdom to be established:	Matthew 6:10
-For relief from affliction:	James 5:13
-For unity in the Body of Christ:	John 17:20-21
-For the persecuted church around the world:	Hebrews 13:3

INTERCEDING WITH THE PROMISES

God answers prayer according to His will and His will is revealed in the promises recorded in His Word.   When you do not ask on the basis of these promises your prayer is not answered.

Ye ask, and receive not, because ye ask amiss, that ye may consume it upon your lusts.   (James 4:3)

It is similar to how a father relates to his children. No parent commits to give his youngsters anything they want or ask for. He makes it clear that he will do certain things and not do other things. Within these limits the father answers his child's requests.

It is the same way with God.   He has given promises and they form the proper basis for prayer. Learn what God has promised and pray according to these promises. One way to do this is to go through the Bible and mark all the promises of God and then base your prayers upon these promises. When you pray a promise, you actually declare God's Word back to Him.   Here is an example:

"Thank you God that you know what is needed even before I ask (Matthew 6:8). I come to you in the name of Jesus, recognizing the power in that name (John 14:14).   I pray for laborers for the harvest to be raised up to extend the Kingdom of God (Matthew 9:37-38)...." etc.

Here are a few examples of Biblical promises.   These promises focus specifically on the subject of prayer:

-The Father knows what you need even before you ask: Matthew 6:8
-If any two agree in prayer, it will be answered: Matthew 18:19
-All things are possible with God: Matthew 19:26; Luke 18:27

-Prayer combined with faith is effective: Matthew 21:22; Mark 11:24
-If you ask in the name of Jesus, it will be done: John 14:14

-The effectual fervent prayer of the righteous avails much: James 5:16

---

[1] Principles for effective intercession were adapted from the *1992 Personal Prayer Diary,* (Seattle, Washington: Youth With A Mission, 1991), 16.

1.   Write the Key Verse from memory.

____

____

2.   How does a person intercede in prayer?

____

____

3.   For what should we intercede in prayer?

____

____

4.   Summarize some of the principles for effective intercession which you learned in this chapter.

____

____

____

5.   Explain how you can use the promises of God to intercede in prayer.

____

____

(Answers to tests are provided at the conclusion of the final chapter in this manual.)

FOR FURTHER STUDY

World leaders in intercessory prayer have recently used a strategy called "spiritual mapping" to pray for cities and nations. In essence, "spiritual mapping" is an attempt to see a city or a nation or the world as it really is, and not as it appears to be. This tactic is based on the assumption that spiritual reality lies behind the natural. It takes seriously the distinction between the visible and the invisible, superimposing our understanding of forces and events in
the spiritual domain on places and circumstances in the material world.

Spiritual mapping acknowledges that behind many visible aspects of the world around us are spiritual forces, invisible areas of reality, that have more ultimate significance than the visible. Spiritual mapping involves identifying and naming the spiritual forces at work in our communities, cities, and nations, and then applying this knowledge in strategic-level spiritual warfare praying.

The Scriptural mandate for spiritual mapping is taken from when God spoke to the prophet Ezekiel and said:

> **"You also, son of man, take a clay tablet and lay it before you, and portray on it a city, Jerusalem."   (Ezekiel 4:1)**

Ezekiel was to draw a map on a piece of clay. God then told him to "lay siege against it." This is obviously not a reference to physical warfare, but to spiritual warfare.   He was then to take an iron plate and put it between him and the city as if it were a wall and he was to lay siege against that as well.

There are many levels of spiritual mapping. Mapping could be done in your neighborhood or your particular section of the city. Mapping could be done for the city as a whole, for the city and its surrounding area, for the state or the province, or for the entire nation. Some will want to map clusters of nations.

There are two parts to spiritual mapping: First, you gather the information. Second, you pray about what you discover. You can locate information by visiting the local library, historical museums, the chamber of commerce, consulting old copies of the local newspaper, or conversing with elderly residents and members of the historical society for your city (if one exists).

The following summary of guidelines will assist you in naming and mapping the spiritual forces at work in your own city:

OBJECTIVES OF SPIRITUAL MAPPING:

1.   To identify the enemy's plans, strategies, and plots for a specific geographical area.

2.	To apply this knowledge in intelligent strategic-level warfare prayer and be victorious in a minimum of time with minimum risk and loss.

HISTORICAL RESEARCH:

**A.	The founding of the city**

1.	Who were the people who founded the city?

2.	What was their personal or corporate reason for founding the city? What were their beliefs and philosophies? What was their vision for the future of the city?

3.	What is the significance of the original name of the city? Has the name been changed? Are there other names or popular designations for the city? Do these names have meaning? Are they linked to religion of any sort? Are they demonic or occult names? Do they signify blessing or curses?

**B.	The later history of the city**

1.	What role has the city played in the life and character of the nation as a whole?

2.	As prominent leaders have emerged in the city, what was their vision for their city?

3.	Have any radical changes taken place in the government or political leadership of the city?

4.	Have there been significant or sudden changes in the economic life of the city? Famine? Depression? Technology? Industry? Discovery of natural resources?

5.	What significant immigration has occurred? Was there ever an imposition of a new language or culture on the city as a whole?

6.	How have immigrants or minorities been treated? How have races or ethnic groups related to one another? Have city laws legitimized racism of any kind?

7.	Have city leaders broken any treaties, contracts or covenants?

8.	Have any wars directly affected the city? Were any battles fought in the city? Was there bloodshed?

9.	How has the city treated the poor and oppressed? Has greed characterized city leaders? Is there evidence of corruption among political, economic, or religious leaders and institutions?

10.   What natural disasters have affected the city?

11.   Does the city have a motto or slogan? What is its meaning?

12.   What kinds of music do the people listen to? What is the message they receive from that music?

13.   What five words would most people in the city use to characterize the positive features of their city today?   What five words would they use for the negative features?

HISTORY OF RELIGION IN THE CITY:

A.   Non-Christian religion

1.   What were the religious views and practices of the people who inhabited the area before the city was founded?

2.   Were religious considerations important in the founding of the city?

3.   Have any non-Christian religions entered the city in significant proportions?

4.   What secret orders (such as Freemasonry) have been present in the city?

5.   What witches' covens, Satanist groups, or other such cults have operated in the city?

B.   Christianity

1.   When, if ever, did Christianity enter the city?   Under what circumstances?

2.   Have any of the early or later Christian leaders been Freemasons?

3.   What role has the Christian community played in the life of the city as a whole?   Have there been changes in this?

4.   Is Christianity in the city growing, on a plateau, or declining?

C.   Relationships

1.   Has there been conflict between religions in the city?

2.   Has there been conflict between Christians?

3.   What is the history of the church splits in the city?

PHYSICAL RESEARCH:

1.   Locate different maps of the city, especially the older ones. What changes have taken place in the physical characteristics of the city?

2.   Who were the city planners who designed the city?

3.   Are there any significant discernible designs or symbols imbedded in the original plan or layout of the city?

4.   Is there any significance in the architecture, location, or positional relationship of the central buildings, especially those representing the political, economic, educational, or religious powers in the city?

5.   Has there been any historical significance in the particular plot of land upon which one or more of these buildings are located?   Who originally owned this land?

6.   What is the background of the city's parks and plazas? Who commissioned and funded them? What significance might their names have?

7.   What is the background and possible significance of the statues and monuments of the city? Do any reflect demonic characteristics or glorify the creature rather than the Creator?

8.   What other art work is featured in the city, especially on or in public buildings, museums, or theaters? Look especially for sensual or demonic art.

9.   Are there any prominent archaeological sites in the city?   What meaning might they have?

10.   What is the location of highly visible centers of sin such as abortion clinics, pornographic bookstores or theaters, areas of prostitution, gambling, taverns, homosexual activities, etc.

11.   Where are areas that concentrate greed, exploitation, poverty, discrimination, violence, disease or frequent accidents?

12.   Where are locations of past or present bloodshed through massacre, war, or murder?

13.   Does the position of trees, hills, stones, or rivers form any apparently significant pattern?

14.   Do certain landmarks of the city have names that would not glorify God?

15.   What is the highest geographical point in the city and what is built or located there? This can be a statement of authority.

16.   Which zones or sectors or neighborhoods of your city seem to have characteristics of their own.   Attempt to discern areas of the city that seem to have different spiritual environments.

SPIRITUAL RESEARCH:

A.   Non-Christian

1.   What are the names of the principal deities or territorial spirits associated with the city past or present?

2.   What are the locations of high places, altars, temples, monuments or buildings associated with witchcraft, occult, fortune-telling, Satanism, Freemasonry, Mormonism, eastern religions, Jehovah's witnesses, and the like.   Do these form any pattern when plotted on a map?

3.   What are the sites of pagan worship from the past, even before the city was founded?

4.   What are the different cultural centers that might contain art or artifacts connected with pagan worship?

5.   Has any city leader knowingly dedicated himself or herself to a pagan god or a principality?

6.   Were any known curses placed by the original inhabitants on the land or people who founded the city?

B.   Christian

1.   How have God's messengers been received by the city?

2.   Has evangelism been easy or hard?

3.   Where are the churches located?   Which of them would you see as "life giving" churches?

4.   What is the health of the churches in the city?

5.   Who are the Christian leaders considered as "elders of the city"?

6.   Is it easy to pray in all areas of the city?

7.   What is the status of unity among Christian leaders across ethnic and denominational lines?

8.   What is the view of city leaders toward Christian morality?

C.   Revelational

1.   What are the recognized, mature intercessors hearing from God concerning the city?

2.   What is the identity of the ranking principalities seemingly in control of the city as a whole or certain areas of the city's life or territory?

Now...Use the information you have obtained to pray over your neighborhood, city, or nation. Pray specifically against the evil spiritual forces you have identified.

CHAPTER FIVE

HINDRANCES TO EFFECTIVE INTERCESSION

OBJECTIVES:

Upon completion of this chapter you will be able to:

- Identify and eliminate hindrances to effective intercession.
- Know when not to pray.

KEY VERSE:

Ye ask and receive not because ye ask amiss, that ye may consume it upon your lusts. (James 4:3)

INTRODUCTION

If you want to intercede properly you must identify hindrances to effective intercession and eliminate these from your life. A "hindrance" is anything that stands in your way, preventing you from interceding.

HINDRANCES TO EFFECTIVE INTERCESSION

Study the following Scriptures which reveal hindrances to effective intercession:

-Sin of any kind:	Isaiah 59:1-2; Psalm 66:18; Isaiah 1:15; Proverbs 28:9
-Idols in the heart:	Ezekiel 14:1-3
-An unforgiving spirit:	Mark 11:25; Matthew 5:23
-Selfishness, wrong motives:	Proverbs 21:13; James 4:3
-Power hungry, manipulative prayers:	James 4:2-3
-Wrong treatment of marriage partner:	I Peter 3:7
-Self-righteousness:	Luke 18:10-14
-Unbelief:	James 1:6-7
-Not abiding in Christ and His Word:	John 15:7
-Lack of compassion:	Proverbs 21:13
-Hypocrisy, pride, meaningless repetition:	Matthew 6:5; Job 35:12-13
-Not asking according to the will of God:	James 4:2-3
-Not asking in Jesus' name:	John 16:24
-Satanic demonic hindrances:	Daniel 10:10-13; Ephesians 6:12

-Not seeking first the Kingdom: Only when you seek
first the Kingdom are you promised the "other things":   Matthew 6:33
-When you do not know how to pray as you should,
prayer is hindered. This is why it is important to let
the Holy Spirit pray through you: Romans 8:26

ELIMINATING HINDRANCES TO INTERCESSION

Remember that identifying hindrances to intercession is not enough, but you must also ask God
to help you to eliminate them from your life. Also remember that what seems to be unanswered
prayer does not mean there are hindrances in your life. As we mentioned in Chapter One,
answers to prayer may be delayed (Luke 18:7) or answered differently from our desires (II
Corinthians 12:8-9).

WHEN NOT TO PRAY

It is important to learn how to wait and intercede before the Lord in prayer for His guidance and
direction before acting.   It is equally important to know when not to pray.   Sometimes your
prayer of intercession will result in God calling you to action instead of more prayer.

This is illustrated by the story of Israel at the bitter waters of Marah where they desperately
needed water, but could not drink from this poison stream. When Moses cried unto the Lord in
intercession, God showed him exactly what to do to sweeten the waters. There was no need to
wait further on the Lord in prayer. Moses was to act upon what God had revealed. The same was
true of Joshua when he interceded for Israel about the terrible defeat they suffered at Ai.   God
revealed there was sin among the people and He actually told Joshua...

> **Get thee up; wherefore liest thou thus upon thy face? Israel hath sinned...Up,
> sanctify the people...(Joshua 7: portions of 10,12, and 13)**

It was not the time to pray but it was time to act upon the direction given in prayer.   Some
people use intercession as an excuse to avoid doing what God has told them to do. Powerful
intercession leads to dynamic, effective action. Some people continue to intercede when God has
already answered but they did not like the answer. Review the story of Balaam in Numbers 22.
Note especially verses 18-19. Balaam had no right to go to God with the same matter because
God had already answered him (see verse 12).

1.   Write the Key Verse from memory.

____

____

____

____

2.   List some of the hindrances to effective intercession which were discussed in this chapter.

____

____

____

____

3.   When should you not pray?

____

____

(Answers to tests are provided at the conclusion of the final chapter in this manual.)

FOR FURTHER STUDY

List the hindrances to effective intercession discussed in this chapter.   Put a check mark by any that might be hindering your prayers.   How can you eliminate these hindrances in your life?

CHAPTER SIX

USING THE MODEL PRAYER TO INTERCEDE

OBJECTIVES:

Upon completion of this chapter you will be able to:

* Provide the Scriptural references for both versions of the model prayer.
* Explain why the Lord's prayer is actually a prayer of intercession.
* Recite the model prayer from memory.
* Use the model prayer as a guide for intercession.

KEY VERSES:

> **Our Father in heaven,**
> **Hallowed be Your name.**
> **Your kingdom come,**
> **Your will be done.**
> **On earth as it is in heaven.**
> **Give us this day our daily bread.**
> **And forgive us our debts,**
> **As we forgive our debtors.**
> **And do not lead us into temptation,**
> **But deliver us from the evil one.**
> **For Yours is the kingdom and the power and the glory forever.   Amen.**
> **(Matthew 6:9-13)**

INTRODUCTION

There are two versions of what is called the "Lord's Prayer" or the "model prayer."   One is recorded in Matthew 6:9-13 and one in Luke 11:2-4.   Most Bible scholars agree that the similarities between them justify regarding the two versions as forms of the same prayer rather than different prayers.

Matthew's version was given when Jesus taught the Sermon on the Mount. The passage in the book of Luke was given about two and a half years later when the disciples came to Jesus asking Him to teach them to pray. During this interim period, the disciples watched Jesus pray and witnessed the power that resulted from His prayer experiences.   This created in the Disciples a yearning desire to learn to pray, so they asked their Master, "Teach us to pray."

Jesus responded with the words of what has come to be called the "Lord's prayer":

> **In this manner, therefore, pray:**
> **Our Father in heaven,**
> **Hallowed be Your name.**
> **Your kingdom come,**
> **Your will be done.**
> **On earth as it is in heaven.**
> **Give us this day our daily bread.**
> **And forgive us our debts,**
> **As we forgive our debtors.**
> **And do not lead us into temptation,**
> **But deliver us from the evil one.**
> **For Yours is the kingdom and the power and the glory forever.   Amen.**
> **Matthew 6:9-13**

A PRAYER OF INTERCESSION

When the disciples came to Jesus, they said "Teach us to pray," not "Teach us a prayer." Jesus responded to their request by using a method commonly employed by the Jewish rabbis.   The rabbis often listed certain topics of truth, then under each point provided a complete outline.

In this model prayer, Jesus used this same teaching pattern. He gave topics and instructed, "After this manner, therefore, pray."   "After this manner, therefore, pray" (*houtos oun* in the Greek text) means "pray along these lines." Jesus did not command His followers to repeat the prayer word for word, but rather to pray "after this manner."

His prayer began with the plural possessive pronominal adjective "our." Further in the prayer we see statements like "give us," "lead us," and "forgive us." In every sense, the model prayer is an intercessory prayer because you pray for others as well as yourself.

ANALYSIS OF THE PRAYER

The following is a brief analysis of this model intercessory prayer:

OUR FATHER WHICH ART IN HEAVEN:

The words " Our Father" indicate nearness, but the words "in Heaven" imply distance.   Psalms 139 reveals, however, that God is everywhere. When we pray to "Our Father in Heaven," it does not emphasize the distance between us and the Father, but it immediately brings us from the natural world to a powerful spiritual plane.   It assures us that God has at His disposal the entire resources of the supernatural realm with which to respond to the requests presented in the remainder of the model prayer. When we pray "Our Father in Heaven,"   we are immediately linked through Christ with a supernatural God with unlimited supernatural resources that can be used in intercessory prayer.

HALLOWED BE YOUR NAME:

When we become members of God's family, our Heavenly Father's name is given to us just as a child who is adopted in the natural world assumes the name of his new Dad. Our spiritual adoption gives us the right to call God "Father" and receive all the benefits associated with His Name because we are now heirs of our Father's Kingdom.

God's name is not just an identification label but it is an expression of His nature and identity. When we say "Hallowed be Your Name" we proclaim the person, power, and authority of God. When you pray for others, you can use these names to intercede for God to work in their lives. Here is an example:

> *"I pray for my wife, that you will be Jehovah-shalom to her.   I pray that you will be her Jehovah-jireh, providing her every need this day.   Jehovah-nissi, I pray that your banner will reign over her life.   I pray that as Jehovah-m'kaddesh you will sanctify her this day... (etc.)"*

The following list identifies the seven compound names of God and their meanings:

NAME	MEANING	REFERENCE
Jehovah-tsidkenu	Jehovah Our Righteousness	Jeremiah 23:6
Jehovah-m'kaddesh	Jehovah Who Sanctifies	Exodus 31:13
Jehovah-shalom	Jehovah Is Peace	Judges 6:24
Jehovah-shammah	Jehovah Is There	Ezekiel 48:35
Jehovah-rophe	Jehovah Heals	Exodus 15:26
Jehovah-jireh	Jehovah My Provider	Genesis 22:14
Jehovah-nissi	Jehovah My Banner	Exodus 17:15
Jehovah-rohi	Jehovah My Shepherd	Psalms 23:1

YOUR KINGDOM COME:

In Greek, Hebrew, and Aramaic the "Kingdom" of God refers to the kingship, sovereignty, reign, or ruling activity of God. It is the expression of God's nature in action.

God's realm of operation can be viewed in terms of its inclusive universal organization as the Kingdom of God; its local visible organization as the Church through which the Kingdom is extended; and individuals of which the Kingdom is composed, that is, all true believers born into this Kingdom.

Sometime in the future the Kingdom of God will be established in visible form. We do not know the exact timing of this (Acts 1:7), but according to the Word of God it is certain. All the "kingdoms of the world" will become the property of God, the evil Kingdom of Satan will be defeated, and our King will reign forever (Revelation 11:15).

The centrality of the Kingdom message is clear in the New Testament record. It is mentioned some 49 times in Matthew, 16 times in Mark, and 38 times in Luke. Jesus began His earthly ministry by declaring the arrival of the Kingdom (Matthew 4:17). He ended His earthly ministry by speaking of things pertaining to the Kingdom (Acts 1:3). In between the beginning and end of His earthly ministry, the emphasis was always on the Kingdom.   He was constantly declaring He must preach its message in other places (Luke 4:43). Every parable of Jesus related to the Kingdom and His life patterned its principles.

Jesus indicated that we, as believers, were to give similar emphasis to the Kingdom:

> **"But seek first the kingdom of God and His righteousness, and all these things shall be added to you. "   (Matthew 6:33)**

This verse indicates where we should focus our praying, preaching, teaching, and living.   It should all be targeted on the Kingdom of God.   If we "seek first the Kingdom," it assures the answer to the other petitions that follow in the model prayer.

Praying "Your Kingdom Come" is more than a prayer for the return of Jesus and establishing of the Kingdom in its final form. When we pray "Your Kingdom Come," we are actually declaring that our Father will reign in the lives of believers, unbelievers, and the entire earth. We are interceding that God will be acknowledged as King and that life here on earth may be regulated by His commands.

When we say the words "Your Kingdom come" we are actually asking God to remove anything that is in rebellion against His Kingdom, including words, attitudes, desires, behavior, etc., in ourselves and others.

YOUR WILL BE DONE ON EARTH AS IT IS IN HEAVEN:

In Greek there are two words used for the word "will" in reference to God. One word is *"boulema"*.   This word refers to God's sovereign will which is His predetermined plan for everything that happens in the universe. This type of   "God's will" is fulfilled regardless of decisions made by man. It is His master plan for the world and God is at work in the world to bring to pass all things on the basis of His sovereign will:

> **In whom also we have obtained an inheritance, being predestined according
> to the purpose of Him who works all things according to the counsel of His
> will. (Ephesians 1:11)**

The "boulema" will of God does not require the cooperation of man. In the "boulema" will of God, the outcome is predetermined. The "boulema" will of God is written in His Word and is quite clear. There is no need to seek this will of God because it is revealed in the Bible.

The other word for God's will is *"thelema"* and it refers to His individual plan or will for each man and woman. In order for God to fulfill His "thelema" will, it requires man's cooperation. People have the power to choose whether or not they will walk in the "thelema" will of God. When you pray "Your will be done" over yourself or another person, you are interceding for that "thelema" will of God to be done.

GIVE US THIS DAY OUR DAILY BREAD:

In the model prayer, we seek first the Kingdom when we declare "Your Kingdom come" over every circumstance in our lives. We submit in righteousness to our Heavenly Father's will, declaring "Your will be done." Now we can pray with assurance, "Give us this day our daily bread," asking that our needs be met to enable us to fulfill His will and extend His Kingdom.

"Give us" acknowledges that God is our source, not a denomination or a company pay check. The Greek word translated "daily" in this model prayer, occurs nowhere else in the Bible. It means "necessary or essential bread, sufficient for our sustenance and support." Its use in this context confirms that the model prayer Jesus taught is to be prayed each day.

The prayer is for "bread" which indicates both spiritual and material sustenance. The word "us" denotes that we intercede for this "daily bread" of provision for others as well as ourselves.

AND FORGIVE US OUR DEBTS, AS WE FORGIVE OUR DEBTORS:

We must learn to both receive and give forgiveness for our own personal offenses and injustices caused to us by others. Personal offenses occur when you offend God through your own sin. You deal with it by asking Him to forgive you when you say, "Forgive us our debts." The Bible declares:

> **If we say that we have no sin, we deceive ourselves, and the truth is not in us.
> If we confess our sins, He is faithful and just to forgive us our sins and to
> cleanse us from all unrighteousness. (I John 1:8-9)**

When you confess your known sin, God forgives your unknown sin as well as what you have confessed, cleansing you from all unrighteousness.

The second area in which forgiveness must be manifested is in forgiving others of direct and indirect offenses.   A direct offense occurs when you are offended by someone. Indirect offenses are when someone hurts a friend or relative and you take up their offense. Jesus taught that we were to deal with such misdeeds by praying "Forgive us our debts, as we forgive our debtors."

The literal rending of this verse in Greek is "as we forgave our debtors." Thus the verse could read, "Forgive us our debts, as we have forgiven others." The idea is that before we ever seek forgiveness for our sins against God, we are to have already forgiven those who have sinned against us. Jesus taught this principle in the parable of the unjust servant in Matthew 18:22-35. This story illustrates that God's forgiveness precedes human forgiveness. Human forgiveness is a reflection of God's forgiveness, and God's forgiveness becomes real for us only when we are willing to forgive one another.

Jesus summarized these truths when He declared:

> **"...If you have anything against anyone, forgive him, that your Father in heaven may also forgive your trespasses.   But if you do not forgive, neither will your Father in heaven forgive your trespasses." (Mark 11:25)**

Satan causes offenses in your family, between friends, in your business relationships, and in your church. The Bible states "offenses will come" (Matthew 18:7). How will you deal with these issues when they arise? Will you intercede about them in prayer or just talk about them through gossip?

**AND DO NOT LEAD US INTO TEMPTATION,
BUT DELIVER US FROM THE EVIL ONE:**

Jesus taught us to pray, "Do not lead us into temptation," but James indicates God does not tempt man:

> **Let no one say when he is tempted, "I am tempted by God"; for God cannot be tempted by evil, nor does He Himself tempt anyone.
> (James 1:13)**

So who is the tempter to whom Jesus is referring? The Bible clearly reveals that this is the role of our enemy, Satan (Matthew 4:3; 1 Thessalonians 3:5). The Scriptures repeatedly warn of temptations which come from the devil (Matthew 4:1; 1 Corinthians 7:5; 1 Thessalonians 3:5). The Bible explains that...

> **...each one is tempted when he is drawn away by his own desires and enticed. Then, when desire has conceived, it gives birth to sin; and sin, when it is full-grown, brings forth death.   (James 1:14-15)**

Satan is the tempter, but we are drawn into his snare when we allow our fleshly desires to entice us.   Such desires birth sin, and sin results in death. Some of Satan's attacks arise from uncontrolled evil passions from within, while other temptations come from without through our senses of hearing, seeing, feeling, touching, and tasting.   Whatever their source, the Apostle Paul assures us:

> **No temptation has overtaken you except such as is common to man; but God is faithful, who will not allow you to be tempted beyond what you are able, but with the temptation will also make the way of escape, that you may be able to bear it.   (I Corinthians 10:13)**

When we pray, "Do not lead us into temptation," we are asking God to preserve us from the enticement to sin. Even Jesus was not delivered from temptation, but was preserved in it (Hebrews 4:15). The Apostle John assures us:

> **We know (absolutely) that any one born of God does not (deliberately and knowingly) practice committing sin, but the One Who was begotten of God carefully watches over and protects him-Christ's divine presence within him preserves him against the evil-and the wicked one does not lay hold (get a grip) on him or touch (him).   (I John 5:18 Amplified Version)**

In Ephesians 6:10-18, the Apostle Paul provides detailed information about the evil one and the spiritual armor which God provides for our defense. Paul emphatically declares we should be strong in the Lord and in the power of His might and stand boldly in the face of these evil forces (Ephesians 6:10,11,13). He decrees that it is possible to stand against every wile   (deceit, cunning, craftiness) of the devil. Paul admonishes that we should war a good warfare (I Timothy 1:18), fight an effective fight of faith (I Timothy 6:12), and battle intelligently with purpose (I Corinthians 9:26).

Paul emphasizes that the battle is not a natural one and natural weapons are ineffective. Spiritual battles must be fought with spiritual weapons:

> **Therefore take up the whole armor of God, that you may be able to withstand in the evil day, and having done all to stand,**
>
> **Stand therefore, having girded your waist with truth, having put on the breastplate   of righteousness,   and having shod your feet with the preparation of the gospel of peace,**
>
> **Above all, taking the shield of faith with which you will be able to quench all the fiery darts of the wicked one.**

And take the helmet of salvation, and the sword of the Spirit, which is the word of God.

Praying always with all prayer and supplication in the Spirit being watchful to this end with all perseverance and supplication for all the saints...(Ephesians 6:13-18)

The purpose of the armor is to be able to stand against the wiles of the enemy, Satan.   Paul commands you to "put on" this spiritual armor which means it is your responsibility to appropriate what God has provided. To "put on" means you take hold of something and apply it to yourself. Here is how to do it as you intercede each day for yourself and others:

Armor	Declaration To Make	Promise To Claim	Opposite Spirit To Bind
Loins girded with truth	Jesus, You are my truth.	John 14:6	Deception
Breastplate of righteousness	Jesus, You are my righteousness.	II Corinthians 5:21	Unrighteousness
Feet shod with the preparation of the Gospel	Jesus, You are my readiness.	Philippians 4:13	Lethargy
The shield of faith	Jesus, You are my faith.	Galatians 2:20	Unbelief, doubt
Helmet of salvation	Jesus, You are my salvation.	Hebrews 5:9	Vain imaginations Evil thoughts
Sword of the Spirit (Word	Jesus, You are my living Word.	John 1:14	Lies of Satan

FOR YOURS IS THE KINGDOM AND THE POWER AND THE GLORY FOREVER:

The word "for" indicates the authority by which the model prayer has been prayed. It means "because" the kingdom, power, and glory belong to God, we can claim the provisions, promises, and protection of this prayer. When we arrive at this final portion of the model prayer and declare "Yours is the Kingdom," we are coming into agreement with everything God says about His Kingdom:

"Do not fear, little flock, for it is your Father's good pleasure to give you the kingdom." (Luke 12:32)

It is His Kingdom, but as heirs, it is our Kingdom also. It is a legacy conferred by our Father and it pleases Him to give it to us.

The word for power is *"dunamis"* from which the English words "dynamic" and "dynamite come."   When we end our prayer with "Yours is the power," we are acknowledging the dynamic power of God with its dynamite-like potential for fulfilling our petitions. When we declare, "Yours is the power," God echoes back to us the words of Jesus, "I give you power over all the power of the enemy." This assures an answer to all you have interceded for in the model prayer.

We then declare, "Yours is the glory!" "Glory" is one of the richest words of the English language. No single word can serve as a good synonym, but here are some words that describe it: Honor, praise, splendor, radiance, power, exaltation, worthiness, likeness, beauty, renown, and rank. Jesus said:

> **"And the glory which you gave Me, I have given them that they may be one just as We are one." (John 17:22)**

The same glory with which Jesus was glorified by the Father is a gift to you. All you have to do is claim it. You should be going from "glory to glory" not from defeat to defeat. You may be discouraged and despondent and feel cold and lifeless spiritually, but the Word of the Lord to you today is...

> **Arise from the depression and prostration in which circumstances have kept you; rise to a new life.   Shine, be radiant with the glory of the Lord; for your light is come, and the glory of the Lord is risen upon you.**
> **(Isaiah 60:1-2, The Amplified Version)**

God's glory guarantees:

-Provision:	Philippians 4:19; Ephesians 3:16
-Strength:	Colossians 1:11
-Joy:	Isaiah 66:5; 1 Peter 1:8; II Chronicles 16:10
-Liberty:	Isaiah 60:1
-Rest:	Isaiah 11:10
-Sanctification:	Exodus 29:43
-Unity with other believers:	John 17:22

This word means exactly what it says..."forever" that is "eternal, having no end."   As you conclude your prayer, you are ascribing the Kingdom, power and glory to your Father...*forever.* You are linking yourself in an eternal bond with your Father because you are acknowledging that you share in His Kingdom, power, and glory.

AMEN:

When we use the word "Amen," it seals our prayer with powerful authority because "Amen" is one of the names of Christ (Revelation 3:14).   Christ is called the "Amen of God," for all of God's promises are fulfilled in Him.   When we say "Amen" it means we have prayed all our petitions in the name of Jesus.

The word "Amen" does not mean "over and out...I'm done praying!"   The meaning of this word is, "Even so, as I have prayed it, even so shall it be done," so when you say "Amen" you are actually making a declaration of faith.

SELF-TEST

1.   Write the Key Verses (the Lord's prayer) from memory.

____

____

____

____

____

2.   Where are the two versions of the model prayer located in the Bible?

____

3.   Why is the Lord's Prayer actually a prayer of intercession?

____

____

4.   How can you use the model prayer for intercession?

____

____

5.   How can you use the names of God to intercede for others?

____

____

(Answers to tests are provided at the conclusion of the final chapter in this manual.)

FOR FURTHER STUDY

Praying the promises of the Word of God assures answers to your prayers. Start reading your Bible through and mark each promise either with a certain color or with a "P" in the margin of your Bible.

Begin to use these promises when you pray. You do this by actually praying the promise. For example, here is how you could pray Psalms 9:9-10:

> *"I pray for (name) that You will be a refuge for her/him in the time of trouble. I pray that she will put her trust in You because You, Lord, have not forsaken those that seek You."*

Now...you try it. Select a promise from the Bible and write it below in the form of a prayer:

____

____

____

____

____

____

CHAPTER SEVEN

INTERCEDING FOR REVIVAL

OBJECTIVES

Upon completion of this chapter you will be able to:

- Define revival.
- Explain how we can prepare for revival.
- Recognize when revival is needed.
- Identify evidences of a backslidden condition.
- Summarize Biblical principles of revival.
- Identify obstacles to revival.
- Explain how to use "God's revival plan" to intercede for revival.

KEY VERSE:

If my people, which are called by my name, shall humble themselves, and pray, and seek my face, and turn from their wicked ways; then will I hear from Heaven and will forgive their sin, and will heal their land. (II Chronicles 7:14)

INTRODUCTION

One of the most important tasks of intercession is praying for revival. In this chapter you will learn the definition of revival, how to prepare for it, and how to recognize when it is needed. You will also learn how to identify obstacles that hinder revival and how to intercede for it.

THE DEFINITION OF REVIVAL

First, let us examine what revival is not. Revival is not just emotionalism. People respond emotionally to revival, but emotions are just a part of the revival, they are not the revival. True revival will affect the whole man, however, including his emotions. Knowledge of facts never moves men. Statistics on the number of deaths caused by alcoholic beverage never converts a drunkard. Figures on the increase of crime do not change criminals. The convicting power of the Holy Spirit must touch a man both spiritually and emotionally to effect change.

Revival is not loud music and "hell-fire" preaching. It is not a campaign for new members to increase attendance. Church growth is a result of revival, but it is not the same as revival. Revival is not evangelism. Evangelism is proclaiming the good news of the Gospel. Revival precedes evangelism, for when dead believers are "revived," evangelism results. Finally, revival is not just a series of special meetings...unless those special meetings are touched by the sovereign move of God.

Revival is...

> *"A sovereign, extraordinary work of God through and in behalf of a people who have learned and applied the principles revealed in the rhema Word of God regarding revival."*

Revival is sovereign, in that it cannot be produced by man. It is extraordinary, because it is a special work of God. A revival works within a group of people and in behalf of them. In order to prepare for revival, we must apply the principles revealed in God's Word regarding revival. Everything the Bible teaches about revival is the "rhema" or "specific" word of God on the subject. We may also say that revival is:

-An awakening, revitalizing, restoring of God's people, a strengthening of those things which remain.

-A return to consciousness or life. That which is revived becomes active and flourishing again.

-The inrush of the Spirit into the body that has threatened to become a corpse.

-Times of refreshing from the presence of the Lord. (Acts 3:19)

PREPARING FOR REVIVAL

We can compare preparation for revival to the task of farming. A farmer can sit around and pray for a good harvest, but if he does not prepare the field, plant the seed, and water the crop, it will not come.

Equally foolish is the farmer who thinks because he does his part in these tasks that harvest is assured. It takes the sovereignty of God through rain, sunshine, and the proper weather patterns to bring the crop to maturity. The farmer works in cooperation with the principles of sowing and reaping, seed time and harvest revealed in God's Word. God is still sovereign, for the rain, sun, and proper weather patterns come from Him.

The same analogy may be used for revival. It is a sovereign move of God, but to "reap" revival, we must prepare for it by following the principles revealed in God's Word. Revival is the joint move of the Spirit of God and the response of the people of God.

WHEN REVIVAL IS NEEDED

Revival is always needed of course, but it is most necessary when a backslidden condition is apparent. To understand backsliding, consider the example of Israel. Jeremiah called the problems of Israel "backsliding" (Jeremiah 1:3-4). The Bible says:

The backslider in heart shall be filled with his own ways.   (Proverbs 14:14)

Turn to Jeremiah chapter 2.   You will note that Israel had...

-Determined God was not as important to them as He had formerly been
 ("I used to"....):   2:5

-Forgot the great things God did for them in former days: 2:6-7

-Even the religious leaders of Israel joined the backsliding hosts. The priests failed to ask, "Where is the Lord?":   2:8

-With God crowded out of their lives, they turned to others things...in this case, idols: 2:11-12; 27-28

-They forsook the true source of spiritual water and began to carve out cisterns that could hold no water. They exchanged living water for stagnant water: 2:13

-They began to drift spiritually: 2:19

-They entered into a self-righteous condition: 2:22-23

-They justified themselves with excuses: 3:11

-They drew others into their corruption: 2:33-34

Backsliding is the sin of crowding God out and filling one's life with self.   It is described as a pig going back to the mire and a dog returning to its vomit. (II Peter 2:21-22)

EVIDENCES OF A BACKSLIDDEN CONDITION

Here are some evidences of a backslidden condition. Examine your own heart and life as you study this list. You are entering into a backslidden condition...

1.	When prayer ceases to be a vital part of your life. It has been said that "revival delays because prayer decays."

2.   When the quest for Biblical truth ceases and you become content with the knowledge you have already acquired. This is not to say backsliders do not read the Bible. Many of them have habits of dutiful devotions, but while they read the words the knowledge acquired is treated as facts and not applied to their lives.

3.   When thoughts about eternal things cease to be regular and/or important.

4.   When you pardon your sin with self-righteousness by saying "the Lord knows I am just dust" or "that is the way I am."

5.   When pointed spiritual discussions are an embarrassment and make you uncomfortable.

6.   When things like recreation, sports, and entertainment become first in your life.

7.   When you can indulge in sin without protest by your conscience.

8.   When aspirations of Christ-like holiness are no longer dominant in your life.

9.   When the acquisition of money and goods becomes dominant in your thinking.

10.   When you can hear the Lord's name taken in vain, spiritual concerns mocked, and eternal issues flippantly treated and not be moved to indignation and action.

11.   When "worship" becomes a weariness. Church services lose their excitement, you can mouth religious songs and words without heart, there is no song in your heart, no praise with the ring of joy.

12.   When breaches of unity in the fellowship are of no concern to you.

13.   When the slightest excuse seems sufficient to keep you from Christian service.

14.   When your fleshly senses are out of control: You watch degrading movies and television, listen to ungodly music, and read morally debilitating literature.

15.   When you adjust happily to the world's lifestyle: For examples, unpaid debts, bankruptcy, lying, dishonesty, unkept appointments and promises, immodest styles of dress, cheating your employer of a full day's work, etc.

16.   When your lack of spiritual power no longer concerns you; there is no restless yearning for more of God and His power in your life.

17.   When your church has fallen into spiritual decline, the Word of God is   no longer preached with power in your church and yet you are content.

18.   When the moral, political, spiritual, and economic conditions of the world and your
        nation are of no concern to you.

19.   When your heart is hard: Your tears do not flow easily, you are uncaring, abrupt, etc.
        You do not weep over the things which Jesus wept like a lost city, the spiritual condition
        of man, the sorrows of others.

20.   When you have lost your spiritual strength, and do not even realize it.

BIBLICAL PRINCIPLES OF REVIVAL

Old Testament revivals yield Biblical principles that guide us in praying for revival.   No two
revivals are identical, but the following principles are evident in the Old Testament record:

1.   Most Old Testament revivals were preceded by a time of deep spiritual decline and
        despair.   When conditions are declining around you and you are tempted to despair,
        rejoice instead...You may be on the brink of revival!

2.   Each revival began in the heart of one man, who became the instrument God used to stir
        others.   As God touches your heart with the fire of revival, you will fan the revival flame
        in others.

3.   Every Old Testament revival rested on the powerful proclamation of the Word of God.
        The message of revival should focus on sin, Hell, and God's judgment not just power,
        love, peace, and prosperity.   Consider the revival message of Moses (Deuteronomy
        11:26-28); Samuel (I Samuel 7:3); Ezekiel (Ezekiel 33:7-8); and Elijah (I Kings 18:21).

4.   Repenting from sin always preceded revival: Repentance included the destruction of
        every idol and separation from the world.

5.   There was a return to proper priorities including concern for others, keeping the Sabbath,
        giving, prayer, and the Word of God.

6.   There was a return to the genuine worship of God. This worship was not cold and formal
        ritual, but an exciting, emotional response of the people to their Lord.

7.   Every revival was followed by a time of productivity, prosperity, great joy, and gladness.

OBSTACLES TO REVIVAL

Here are some things that prevent the sovereign move of God in a church:

LEADERSHIP HINDRANCES:

Leaders who do not preach and teach the Word of God in power hinder revival. Those who have no prayer life, no Bible study program, no demonstration of power, and no passion for delivery of the Word hinder revival. Those who control their congregations and quench the spirit of God also hinder His sovereign move.

Leaders who do not really care for the sheep hinder revival. They do not lead the flock to the green pastures and still waters necessary to revive them. Leaders who have lost their compassion for a dying world hinder revival. Many do not recognize their responsibility to be the leaders in revival (Joel 2:15-18).

CONGREGATIONAL HINDRANCES:

There can also be obstacles to revival in the congregation of God's people.   A congregation's love of tradition interferes with revival. Revival and change are synonymous. God is orderly and dependable, but He is also fresh and vital. He is not a traditionalist. If the church must run according to traditions of men, it will run without the power and presence of God.

A congregation's love of formal order hinders revival. Michal, David's wife, condemned him because of his emotional worship and was struck barren. A barren church loves formal order and ritual. Love of brevity also hinders revival. We want God to send revival in the two hours we designate to Him on Sunday morning.

Many congregations love comfortable truth.   They do not want to be confronted with the claims of Christ upon them or preaching about sin and judgment. The truths necessary for revival are not always comfortable.   Love of respect by others also hinders revival. Some congregations are more concerned about "what people will think" than about what God thinks.

GENERAL HINDRANCES:

There are other hindrances which may be found in both leadership and the congregation. Iniquity hinders revival, whether it be found in the man in the pew or the pulpit:

> **Behold the Lord's hand is not shortened, that it cannot save; neither His ear heavy, that it cannot hear (our pleas for revival)...**
>
> **But your iniquities have separated between   you and your God, and your sins have hid His face from you, that He will not hear.   (Isaiah 59:1-2)**
>
> **He that covereth his sins shall not prosper; but whoso confesseth and forsaketh them shall have mercy.   (Proverbs 28:13)**

An attitude of resignation that "these are the last days and we can only expect things to get worse and worse" will hinder revival. Inattention to prayer and the Word, refusing to humble self, and refusing to seek the Lord all hinder revival.   Limiting God hinders His sovereign move in our midst:

> **Yea, they turned back and tempted God, and limited the Holy One of Israel. (Psalms 78:41)**

> **And He did not many mighty works there because of their unbelief. (Matthew 13:58)**

Indifference prevents revival. People become indifferent to the claims of Christ and to the needs of others. Insensitivity to our spiritual condition and to the moving of God's Spirit also hinders revival.

GOD'S REVIVAL PLAN

Each of the hindrances we have discussed can be eliminated through intercession because revival comes in response to prayer. Here is how to pray for revival:

> **If my people, which are called by my name, shall humble themselves, and pray, and seek my face, and turn from their wicked ways; then will I hear from Heaven and will forgive their sin, and will heal their land. (II Chronicles 7:14)**

Many important principles of revival are contained in this verse. First, note that God is speaking to His people ("If my people"). He is not talking to sinners, the world, or just anyone in general. God is talking to His people who are "called by His name."   Here is what God's people must do if they are to experience revival:

1. "HUMBLE THEMSELVES":

To humble yourself is to bring yourself low before God (study Leviticus 26:40-41). This humbling includes humbling yourself before God (II Chronicles 34:1-13); His Word (II Chronicles 34:14-28); and His people (II Chronicles 34:29-33).

2. "PRAY":

You are to pray specific prayers of (1) seeking God and (2) turning from your wicked ways. We often "have not" because we "ask not" or we ask amiss. We should ask God to revive us and pray specific prayers of confession and repentance to prepare our hearts for the move of His Spirit.

3. "SEEK MY FACE":

The phrase "seeking God" is used in the following Old Testament passages:

> Exodus 33:7; Deuteronomy 4:29; Ezra 8:22; II Samuel 12:16; 21:1; I Chronicles
> 16:10-11; II Chronicles 7:14; 11:16; 15:4; 20:4; Psalms 105:3-4; 24:6; 27:8;
> 40:17; 69:7; 70:5; Proverbs 28:5; Isaiah 51:1; Jeremiah 29:13; 50:4; Hosea 3:5;
> 5:6-7,15; 7:10; Daniel 9:3; Zephaniah 1:6; Zechariah 8:21; Malachi 3:1.

A review of these passages reveal that seeking the Lord involves:

1. Voluntarily and wholeheartedly turning to God.
2. An inner attitude of commitment to serve Him.
3. A decision to turn away from all evil.
4. A decision to fulfill His will.
5. A commitment to fervent prayer.

Seeking the Lord is the chief means of averting evil (Amos 5:4,14). It is the evidence of true
humility (Zephaniah 2:3). It is the basis for sensing the presence of God (Hosea 5:15). It brings
life (Amos 5:4-6) and it must be done wholeheartedly (Jeremiah 29:12-13).

4. "TURN FROM THEIR WICKED WAYS":

Prayer and seeking God are not enough in themselves. They must be accompanied by true
repentance which is a change in direction. You must turn from your wicked ways towards God.
Repentance is the truth emphasized in all Biblical revivals. It is evident in every Old Testament
revival. The Church began with calls to repentance (Acts 2). The final call in the book of
Revelation is to repentance (Revelation 22:16).

Repentance is a gift from God that enables you to change the direction of your life (Acts 5:29-31;
11:15-18; II Timothy 2:22-26). All men are commanded to repent (Acts 17:30). It is God's will
that all repent (II Peter 3:9) and God works graciously to draw men to repentance (Romans 2:4).
Without repentance you will perish (Luke 13:3,5).   Jesus commanded that repentance and
remission of sins be preached in His name among all nations (Luke 24:47).

Repentance includes turning from sins of omission (things you do not do that you should);
commission (wrong things you do); and presumption (presuming by not seeking counsel from
God and sinning in the process). Repentance also includes turning from "dead works"

(Hebrews 6:1- 3). "Dead works" are any religious acts done to gain merit with God by human
effort.

Dead works can even include worship, tithing, and deeds of kindness. Worship must be in spirit
and truth or it is a dead work. Giving out of constraint, emotionalism, or because you are

embarrassed to have the offering plate pass in front of you is a dead work. Deeds of kindness or ministry done out of obligation or to receive glory are also dead works.

Any work which has no capacity to be made alive by the Spirit of God is a dead work. For example, sharing the Gospel at all times and places to all men without regard to the prompting of the Spirit of God may be casting pearls before swine (Matthew 7:6) and reproving a scorner in vain (Proverbs 9:7-8). Any work which is done in the energy of the flesh and not in the power of the Holy Spirit is a dead work.

You should constantly examine your spiritual condition, your motives, and methods of ministry and repent of acts of omission, commission, presumption, and dead works.

SUMMARY:

Here is what you must do to prepare for revival:

 -Humble yourself
 -Pray
 -Seek God's face
 -Turn from your wicked ways

Here is what God will do in response:

 -"HEAR from Heaven": Respond
 -"FORGIVE their sin": Reconcile
 -"HEAL their land": Restore

SELF-TEST

1. Write the Key Verse from memory.

2. Define revival.

3. How can we prepare for revival?

4. When is revival needed?

5. Summarize some of the evidences of a backslidden condition which were discussed in this chapter.

6. List the Biblical principles of revival given in this chapter.

8.   Give the Scriptural reference for "God's revival plan."______________________

9.   Explain how to use "God's revival plan" to intercede for revival.

____

____

____

(Answers to tests are provided at the conclusion of the final chapter in this manual.)

FOR FURTHER STUDY

References for Old Testament revivals are provided for further study of these principles.   For each spiritual awakening summarize the existing conditions, the awakening factors, and the results of the revival. The first one is done as an example after which to pattern your own research. You can reproduce the form provided at the end of this chapter for your studies.

REVIVAL UNDER JACOB: Genesis 35:1-15

EXISTING CONDITIONS:

1.   The head of the family was out of fellowship with God: From the beginning, Jacob had been a deceiver and conniver. He had promised to serve God while fleeing the wrath of Esau, but soon forgot this promise. Jacob was self-sufficient.   He did not view what he had achieved as coming from God even though he had sought the Lord's blessing. He believed he had attained his blessings himself.   Jacob was materialistic and more concerned about his   possessions and providing for himself and his family than his relationship with God.

2   The structure of his family was not in Biblical order: There was favoritism shown to Joseph. Jacob did not rule his house well and his sons took revenge for the raping of his daughter (Genesis 34). His wives were deceitful, jealous, and conniving.

3.   There was a poor spiritual environment: His wives stole the false gods of their father. His sons murdered, stole, and looted. He and his family were sinful and idolatrous: Genesis 35.

AWAKENING FACTORS:

1.   Some terrible events shocked Jacob to awareness: Genesis 35.

2.   The revival started with the Word of God: Genesis 35:1.

RESULTS:

This revival occurred in the home. If our homes are revived, our churches will be revived!

1.   The family got rid of their idols and purified themselves: Genesis 35:2.
2.   They acknowledged the true God: Genesis 35:3.

3.   They returned to the place of spiritual experience: (Going to Bethel): Genesis   35:3

4.   They set up the altar, repented, and returned to true worship: Genesis   35:7

5.	Their lives were changed: Jacob's name was changed to signify this spiritual change: Genesis 32:24-32

6.	Jacob received a new revelation of God: The Lord announced Himself as "God Almighty" which means the all powerful, the one who is sufficient: Genesis 32:24-32

Now...use the following references and the form at the end of this chapter to continue your study of Old Testament revival principles:

REVIVAL UNDER MOSES:	Exodus 32:1-35; 33:1-23; chapters 34-35

REVIVAL UNDER SAMUEL:	I Samuel 7:1-17

REVIVAL UNDER ELIJAH:	I Kings 17-18

REVIVAL UNDER ASA:	II Chronicles 14-15
and a parallel account in I Kings 15:9-24.

REVIVAL UNDER JEHOSOPHAT:	II Chronicles 20

REVIVAL UNDER HEZEKIAH:	II Chronicles 29:1-36; 30:1-27; 31:1-21

REVIVAL UNDER JOSIAH:	II Chronicles 34:1-33; 35:1-19

REVIVAL UNDER ZERUBBABEL:	Haggai 1; Zechariah 1:1-6

REVIVAL UNDER SOLOMON:	II Chronicles 6-7

REVIVAL UNDER JONAH:	Book of Jonah.

REVIVAL UNDER NEHEMIAH:	Nehemiah 8-10

Old Testament Revivals

REVIVAL UNDER:_______________________________

REFERENCES:_______________________________

EXISTING CONDITIONS:

AWAKENING FACTORS:

RESULTS:

CHAPTER EIGHT

GETTING STARTED AND KEEPING GOING

OBJECTIVES:

Upon completion of this chapter you will be able to:

- Make a plan for organized prayer.
- Create a personal prayer manual.
- Engage in international intercession.
- Identify problems and solutions for getting started and keeping going.
- Transform intercession from discipline to delight.
- Commit yourself to the ministry of intercession.

KEY VERSE:

> **But when you pray, go into your room, and when you have shut your door, pray to your Father who is in the secret place; and your Father who sees in secret will reward you openly.   (Matthew 6:6)**

INTRODUCTION

During our study of intercessory prayer we have learned what it is, the spiritual resources provided to enable us to do it, and how to do this type of praying. We have also considered the model intercessor, the Lord Jesus Christ, and learned to identify and deal with hindrances to effective praying.   This final chapter provides suggestions on how to get started and keep going in this ministry of intercessory prayer.

ORGANIZING FOR PRAYER

If you want to be an effective intercessor then you have time to pray. One way to do this is to plan for regular prayer times individually and with others. The New Testament reveals the following structure for organizing prayer forces:

PERSONAL PRAYER:

Prayer is to be made on an individual basis in private:

> **But when you pray, go into your room, and when you have shut your door, pray to your Father who is in the secret place; and your Father who sees in secret will reward you openly.   (Matthew 6:6)**

Set aside a special time each day for prayer, preferably early in the morning before you begin your day. If you are not a "morning person" then select another time that is more suitable. This is the time when you will perform your priestly ministry of standing before God with praise and worship and between God and man with petitions and intercession. Before you begin to intercede have a time of personal repentance and ask God to cleanse you from all sin. Repentance is foundational to effective intercession.

TWO PRAYING TOGETHER:

Two praying together is the smallest unit of corporate prayer. Its Biblical structure as well as its inherent power is revealed in the following Scripture:

> **Again I say to you that if two of you agree on earth concerning anything that they ask, it will be done for them by My Father in heaven.**
> **(Matthew 18:19)**

Find a friend who wants to be an intercessor and begin to pray regularly together. If you are married you might want to choose your mate. If you have someone praying with you they can help you keep going when you get discouraged.

SMALL GROUPS:

Small groups (sometimes called "prayer cells") consist of more than two individuals joining together in intercession. There is great power when two or three people join together for this purpose:

> **For where two or three are gathered together in My name, I am there in the midst of them.   (Matthew 18:20)**

You might want to meet weekly for prayer with a small group of friends, co-workers, or relatives.

TOTAL CONGREGATIONAL PRAYER:

The entire church should also join together in times of corporate intercession:

> **These all continued with one accord and prayer and supplication...**
> **(Acts 1:14)**

Acts 12:5 reveals that constant intercession was made by the church for Peter when He was in prison.   If you are a pastor it is your responsibility to plan such times of corporate prayer.

CREATING A PERSONAL PRAYER MANUAL

It is helpful to create a personal prayer manual to direct your intercession. Use a notebook with dividers for different sections. You might include sections for:

-Study notes on intercession and fasting.

-Your city, state, and nation: Obtain maps of your city, state, and nation to pray over them. Obtain lists of political and religious officials and pray over them by name.

-Personal intercession: List personal prayer needs for your family, friends and others and intercede for these each day. Record prayers that are answered to encourage yourself in the ministry of intercession.

-Your church: Obtain an organizational chart for your church or a list of the names of the leaders and pray for them each day. Pray for each member of your church by name.

-Your ministry: Intercede for your own personal ministry. If you teach a Bible class, pray for your students. If you are a pastor, pray for each person in your congregation by name. If you are a parent, pray for your children (who are part of your ministry). If you are a missionary or evangelist, pray for open doors for the Gospel, for your converts, disciples, and coworkers.

-International Intercession: Set aside a section for intercession for the nations of the world and the extension of the Kingdom of God. Since Harvestime International Network is focused on world evangelism, we want to link all of our mission efforts together through prayer. Because of this, we provide the following detailed guidelines for international intercession.

INTERNATIONAL INTERCESSION

Here is a special guide to international intercession that may be used individually, in small groups or by the entire church fellowship:

PRAISE GO GOD: (10 minutes)

We enter God's presence by thanksgiving and praise: Psalms 100:4

INTERCESSION FOR THE WORLD IN GENERAL: (10 minutes)

Before you begin to intercede, pray a prayer of personal repentance.   Then pray for the world in general for...

-A new spiritual hunger throughout the world.

-God to raise up a worldwide force of international intercessors.

-The growth and development of the Church all over the world.

-God to   raise up "laborers for the harvest."

-Unity and cooperation among existing churches and missions.

-A revival of zeal and compassion to win the lost.

-Wise use of material resources by believers to spread the Gospel. Ask God to provide the necessary finances and to raise up those willing and capable of funding evangelistic efforts.

-Open "doors of utterance" to share the Gospel (Ephesians 6:19)

-"Closed countries"   to open to the Gospel (II Thessalonians 3:1).

-Receptivity in those who hear the Gospel (Romans 15:30-31).

-Major world issues affecting the spread of the Gospel.

-For the hearts of government and political leaders to be receptive to the work of missions and evangelism.

-Laborers planting new churches and missions.

-Believers who are imprisoned or suffering because of their commitment to Christ or because   of their ministry.

-The work of Bible translators throughout the world.

-Christian correspondence courses, training institutes, and Bible colleges throughout the world.

-National Christian workers.

-The cross-cultural missionary force.

-A move of God among the young people.   They are the future leaders of the Church.

-Revelation of the right strategy to reach each nation and village of the world. Ask God to reveal it to those laboring in these regions. Pray for organizations engaged in mission research and strategy.

-Protection for laborers from the attacks of Satan. Bind the activities of Satan coming against believers and nations. Pray for deliverance from those who oppose the Gospel (Romans 15:30-31; II Thessalonians 3:2).

-The Biblical world view to be spread among believers and that they will become participators instead of spectators of God's plan.

-Those who work in secular occupations in various nations in order to spread the Gospel.

-Believers in armed forces stationed in various regions of the world. They can be an effective force in spreading the Gospel.

-The work of religious media such as Gospel recordings, films, cassette tapes, Christian radio, and television.

-The work of medical, relief, and social missions that combine medical and physical assistance with the spreading of the Gospel.

-Missionary aviation organizations and their dedicated pilots who fly missionaries and supplies to various regions of the world.

-The work among immigrants and refugees of the world.

-The binding of spiritual powers of Satan that are influencing nations and regions. That such powers exist is illustrated by the prince that had power over Persia in the time of Daniel. These powers explain why some nations are more   receptive to the Gospel than others. Certain spirits are active in various regions. Until they are bound these regions will not be receptive to the Gospel.

INTERCESSION FOR ONE AREA OF THE WORLD: (10 minutes)

Use a world map as you pray for the nations. Here are some specific things to pray about for each nation:

-Current events. You can keep aware of specific prayer needs by observing current news events in the nation or by keeping in contact with Christian workers there.

-The churches of the nation.

-Those laboring in the spiritual harvest fields of this nation: Those planting churches, national workers, training institutes, missionaries, Bible translators, etc.

-All believers in this nation.

-Unreached peoples of the nation.

-Binding the powers of Satan operating in this nation; those forces which would come against the spread of the Gospel or close the nation to evangelism efforts.

-In every society there are basically seven areas which shape the thinking of individuals and the destiny of the nation.   These are the home and family, the church, education, arts and entertainment, media, government, and business. Intercede for each of these areas.

INTERCESSION FOR A SPECIFIC MISSIONARY OR AGENCY: (10 minutes)

By keeping in touch with the missionary or agency you will be aware of specific needs for which to pray.   Have your name put on the list to receive their newsletter or prayer bulletin.

PRAYER FOR ONE UNREACHED PEOPLE GROUP: (10 minutes)

The five major unreached people groups are Buddhists, Hindus, tribal peoples, Muslims, and Chinese.

>   -Pray for spiritual hunger among these groups.
>   -Pray for laborers to share the Gospel with them.
>   -Pray for revelation of the proper strategy to reach each individual group.
>   -Pray for those already attempting to reach these people.

PERSONAL PRAYER: (10 minutes)

Consider your own personal needs in relation to the world.   How do your personal needs relate to God's global purpose and your part in it?   Even your most personal concerns should somehow relate to   God's plan for the nations. Seek God for ways you can fulfill your part of the commission to reach the nations of the world with the Gospel of the Kingdom. How can you better equip yourself to do this?   How can you begin right now?   How can you free more of your personal time and finances for the cause of world missions?

PROBLEMS THAT MUST BE OVERCOME

Everyone who has ever prayed effectively faced problems that had to be overcome. Conquering these challenges is part of intercession:

> *"To strive in prayer means to struggle through those hindrances which would*
> *restrain or even prevent us entirely from continuing in persevering prayer.   It*
> *means to be so watchful at all times that we can notice when we become slothful*
> *in prayer and that we go to the Spirit of prayer to have this remedied."*
> *-Dr. O. Hallesby*

Take each problem you face to God who through the "Spirit of prayer " (the Holy Spirit) will help you remedy it.   Here are some common problems you might face:

LACK OF TIME:

We always find time for what we really want to do.   Lack of time is not an excuse. The busier you are the more you need to intercede. Set a time for prayer and do not let anything intrude in that time. Do not base the time you spend in prayer on what others may spend because you may need more or less time depending on the subject matter of your prayer. Intercession does not have to be lengthy to be effective. Consider the effectiveness of the prayer of the thief on the cross ("Remember me when you come into your Kingdom") or the publican's earnest appeal ("Lord be merciful to me a sinner") in contrast to the Pharisee's long, self-righteous prayer.

DISTRACTIONS:

Try to minimize interruptions during intercession. Leave instructions with your mate, secretary or a friend that you are not to be disturbed during this time. If you have a telephone let someone take messages, disconnect it, or use an answering machine. Do not pray where a radio or television set is in use. Soft Christian music in the background sometimes covers other distracting noises like nearby traffic or conversation by others.

TIREDNESS:

If you grow weary or sleepy during prayer time, try walking while you pray or praying out loud.

LACK OF DESIRE:

Desire for the ministry of intercession can be systematically developed. It starts with the discipline of doing it regularly whether you "feel" like it or not. Our entire Christian experience is based on faith, not feeling. When you begin to see the results of intercession in your own life and in the lives of others for whom you are interceding, your prayer time will be transformed from discipline to delight.

> *"For who is it who gives you the desire?   God, of course.   Does He give it you in order that it may stay unfulfilled? That is impossible. He implants within you a desire for something with the intention of giving you that very thing; He will infallibly give it you if you ask for it in the right way...and He assists you to make the petition."   -Jean-Nicholas Grou*

THE BEGINNING OF THE END

We have come to the end of our study on intercession. In reality, however, it is not an end but a beginning. You have just received the most powerful spiritual resource available to the Body of Christ...that of intercession.   Through intercession, you can go spiritually anywhere in the world.

Your prayers can penetrate unreached nations and cross through geographical, cultural and political barriers. You can affect the destiny of individuals and entire nations. You can actually help save lives and souls of men and women, boys and girls.

You have joined in an intimate partnership with God through intercession. You can pray with confidence knowing that:

> **The Lord of hosts hath sworn, saying, Surely as I have thought, so shall it come to pass; and as I have purposed so shall it stand.   (Isaiah 14:24)**

> **This is the purpose that is purposed upon the whole earth; and this is the hand that is stretched out upon all the nations.**

> **For the Lord of hosts hath purposed and who shall disannul it?   and his hand is stretched out, and who shall turn it back?   (Isaiah 14:26-27)**

The Lord of Hosts has a purpose, and no force of the world, flesh, demons, Hell, or Satan himself will impede it. You are now part of that divine purpose through the ministry of intercession.   We close with this powerful description of intercession by Canon Liddon:

> *"Is it true that intercession is simply compliance with habit, dull and mechanical? Let those who have really prayed give the answer.*

> *They sometimes describe prayer with the patriarch Jacob as a wrestling together with an unseen power which may last, not infrequently in an earnest life, late into the night hours, or even to the break of day.   Sometimes they refer to common intercession with Paul as a concerted struggle.*

> *They have, when praying, their eyes fixed on the great intercessor in Gethsemane, upon the drops of blood which fall to the ground in that agony of resignation and sacrifice.*

> *Importunity (persistence) is the essence of successful intercession...it means not dreaminess, but sustained work.   It is through intercession specially that the kingdom of heaven suffereth violence and the violent take it by force."*
> *-Canon Liddon*

Are you ready to make such a commitment?

SELF-TEST

1.   Write the Key Verse from memory.

____

____

2.   Write out your personal prayer plan. When will you start? What time each day will you set for prayer? Where will you pray?

____

____

____

3.   Which problems discussed in this lesson are ones that you may have to overcome to get started in prayer and keep going?

____

____

____

4.   Have you created your personal prayer manual?______ If not, consult the "For Further Study" section of this chapter.

5.   Have you committed yourself to a daily time of intercession?__________

6.   If you are a pastor, teacher or other group leader, write out a prayer plan for involving your congregation, students, or group members in united prayer.

____

____

(Answers to tests are provided at the conclusion of the final chapter in this manual.)

FOR FURTHER STUDY

Here are guidelines to assist you in creating your own personal prayer manual.

SECTION ONE: STUDY NOTES

Insert your personal study notes on intercession and fasting in this section so you can review them frequently.

SECTION TWO: CITY, STATE, NATION

Obtain maps of your city, state, and nation to pray over them.   Obtain lists of political and religious officials and pray over them by name.   Insert the information you obtained through "spiritual mapping" of your neighborhood, city, state, or nation.

SECTION THREE: PERSONAL INTERCESSION

Personal Needs: List personal prayer needs for your family, friends, and others and intercede for these each day.   Record prayers that are answered to encourage yourself in the ministry of intercession.

Your Church: Obtain an organizational chart for your church or a list of the names of the leaders and pray for them each day.   Pray for each member of your church by name.

Your Ministry: Intercede for your own personal ministry.   If you teach a Bible class, pray for your students.   If you are a pastor, pray for each person in your congregation by name.   If you are a parent, pray for your children (who are part of your ministry).   If you are a missionary or evangelist,   pray for open doors for the Gospel, for your converts, disciples, and coworkers.

SECTION FOUR: INTERNATIONAL INTERCESSION

In this section, place a copy of the guidelines for international intercession which were given in this chapter.   You may also want to obtain maps of various nations to include in this section.

APPENDICES

APPENDIX ONE: INDEX OF PRAYERS IN THE BIBLE

You learned in this course that Jesus is the greatest model of intercessory prayer.   There are many other examples of effective intercessors in the Bible.   The following list contains references for all the prayers in the Bible.   Use the study guide provided in this appendix to increase your knowledge of intercessory prayer by studying these prayers and the lives of those who prayed them.

PRAYERS IN THE OLD TESTAMENT

Genesis:

Prayer history begins: 4:26
Prayer and spiritual progress: 5:21-24
Prayer and the altar: 12-13
Prayer for an heir: 15
Prayer, the language of a cry: 16
Prayer and revelation: 17
Prayer for a wicked city: 18-19
Prayer after a lapse: 20
Prayer of obedience: 22
Prayer for a bride: 24
Prayer for a barren wife: 25:19-23
Prayer changes things: 26
Prayer as a vow: 28
Prayer about a wronged brother: 32
Prayer, the hidden fire: 39-41; 45:5-8; 50:20,24
Prayer for blessing upon the tribes: 48-49

Exodus:

Prayer expressed as a groan: 1-2
Prayer as a dialogue: 3-4
Prayer as complaint: 5-7
Prayer in league with omnipotence: 8-10
Prayer as praise: 15
Prayer in peril: 17
Prayer of the needy: 22:22-24
Prayer for delay of deserved judgment: 32
First prayer of Moses for Israel: 32:9-14

Second prayer of Moses: 32:30-34
Third prayer of Moses: 33:12-23
Prayer and transfiguration: 34

Numbers:

Prayer as benediction: 6:24-27
Prayer for preservation and protection: 10:35-36
Prayer for the removal of judgment: 11:1-2
Prayer of a discouraged heart: 11:10-35
Prayer of a meek man: 12
Prayer for the upholding of divine honor: 14
Prayer for divine action against rebellion: 16
Prayer for relief from death: 21
Prayer and prophecy: 23-24
Prayer for a new leader: 27

Deuteronomy:

Prayer for a privileged task: 3:23-29
Prayer to one who is nigh: 4:7
Prayer for the stay of judgment: 9:20,26-29
Prayer as a blessing: 21:6-9
Prayer as thanksgiving: 26
Prayer as a song: 32-33

Joshua:

Prayer as a challenge: 5:13-15
Prayer God does not answer: 7
Prayer neglected with dire results: 9:14
Prayer that produced a miracle: 10

Judges:

Prayer for direction: 1
Prayer in time of war: 4-5
Prayer for signs: 6
Prayer in calamity: 10:10-16
Prayer as a bargain: 11:30-40
Prayer for an unborn child: 13
Prayer in the face of death: 16:28-31
Prayer directly answered: 20:23-28
Prayer for a lost tribe: 21:2-3

I Samuel:

Prayer without words: 1
Prayer, prophetic in outlook: 2:1-10
Prayer in the sanctuary: 3
Prayer for national trouble: 7
Prayer for a king: 8
Prayer as vindication: 12
Prayer of a distressed king: 14
Prayer of a grieved heart: 15:11
Prayer as a still small voice: 16:1-12
Prayer as the secret of courage: 17
Prayer as enquiry: 23
Prayer for deaf ears: 28:7
Prayer for restoration of war-spoil: 30

II Samuel:

Prayer as to possession: 2:1
Prayer for victory signs: 5:19-25
Prayer for blessing upon house and kingdom: 7:18-29
Prayer for a sick child: 12
Prayer as pretense: 5:7-9
Prayer for understanding of affliction: 21:1-12
Prayer as a psalm: 22
Prayer as a confession of pride: 24:10-17

I Kings:

Prayer for a wise heart: 3
Prayer of dedication: 8:12-61
Prayer for a withered hand: 13:6
Prayer for closed skies: 17
Prayer for resurrection of dead son: 17:20-24
Prayer for divine honor: 18:16-41
Prayer and perseverance: 18:45
Prayer for death: 19

II Kings:

Prayer for a dead child: 4:32-37
Prayer for vision: 6:13-17
Prayer for deliverance from defiant foes: 19
Prayer for longer life: 20:1-11

I Chronicles:

Prayer for spiritual prosperity: 4:9-10
Prayer as trust: 5:20
Prayer of fear: 13:12
Prayer for establishment of covenant: 17:16-27
Prayer answered by fire: 21
Prayer as a sentinel: 23:30
Prayer and giving: 29:10-19

II Chronicles:

Prayer in national danger: 14:11
Prayer and reform: 15
Prayer and appeal to history: 20:3-13
Prayer of penitence: 33:13

Ezra:

Prayer of thanksgiving: 7:27-28
Prayer and fasting: 8:21-23
Prayer and confession: 9:5-10:4

Nehemiah:

Prayer born of distress: 1:4-11
Prayer in a tight corner: 2:4
Prayer for deliverance from reproach: 4:1-6
Prayer triumphing over anger: 4:7-9
Prayer and restitution: 5
Prayer against craft: 6:9-14
Prayer and the Word: 8:1-13
Prayer and God's goodness: 9
Prayer for remembrance: 13:14,22,29,31

Job:

Prayer of resignation: 1:20-22
Prayer for pity: 6:8-9; 7:17-21
Prayer for justification: 9
Prayer, Job's against injustice: 10
Prayer for light on immortality: 14:13-22
Prayer and profit: 21:14-34
Prayer and reason: 23
Prayer answered by whirlwind: 38
Prayer as confession: 40:3-5; 42:1-6
Prayer as intercession: 42:7-10

Psalms:

Prayer born of rebellion: 3
Prayer of holiness: 4
Prayer as a morning watch: 5
Prayer for divine action: 7
Prayer of praise for divine action: 8
Prayer for preservation here and hereafter: 16
Prayer of the cross: 22
Prayer for shepherd care: 23
Prayer for the manifestation of divine glory: 24
Prayer as ascent to God: 25
Prayer of a believing heart: 27
Prayer as a cameo of Christ: 31
Prayer of a tragic soul: 32
Prayer for protection against enemies: 35
Prayer in praise of loving kindness: 36
Prayer of a pilgrim: 39, 90, 91
Prayer and its accomplishment: 40
Prayer in deep distress: 41
Prayer as a door of hope: 42-43
Prayer for divine assistance: 44
Prayer for a refuge: 46
Prayer of a broken heart: 51
Prayer at all times: 55
Prayer of distress: 57
Prayer of trust: 71
Prayer for God Himself: 73
Prayer as praise for God's greatness: 96
Prayer for escape from trials: 102-103, 105

Prayer of remembrance: 106
Prayer for those in perils on sea: 107
Prayer and affinity to Scripture: 19, 119
Prayer for searching of heart: 139

Proverbs:

Book focuses on prayers as the channel of wisdom.

Ecclesiastes:

Book discusses prayer and fatalism.

Song of Solomon:

Prayer's secrets.

Isaiah:

Prayer God does not hear: 1:15; 16:12
Prayer and cleansing: 6
Prayer for a sign: 7:11
Prayer of exaltation: 12
Prayer of praise for triumphs: 25
Prayer for peace: 26
Prayer and confidence: 41
Prayer and practice: 55
Prayer unpopular to many: 59
Prayer for display of divine power: 63-64

Jeremiah:

Prayer as confession of inability: 1
Prayer as mourning for backsliding: 2-3
Prayer as complaint: 4:10-31
Prayer of lament over rebellion: 5
Prayer from a prison: 6
Prayer forbidden: 7:16
Prayer for justice: 10:23-25
Prayer of perplexity: 12:1-4
Prayer for relief from sin and drought: 14:7-22
Prayer for divine vengeance: 15:15-21
Prayer for confusion of enemies: 16:19-21; 17:13-18
Prayer for overthrow of evil counsel: 18:18-23

Prayer of a despairing heart: 20:7-13
Prayer of gratitude for divine goodness: 32:16-25
Prayer for a believing remnant: 42

Lamentations:

Prayer of pain: 1:20-22
Prayer for pity: 2:19-22
Prayer as complaint: 3
Prayer for the oppressed: 5

Ezekiel:

Prayer as protest: 4:14
Prayer for preservation of residue: 9:8-11
Prayer sanctuary: 11:13-16

Daniel:

Prayer for interpretation: 2:17-18
Prayer in defiance of decree: 6:10-15
Prayer of confession: 9
Prayer and its spiritual results: 10
Prayer concerning the brevity of life: 12:8-13

Hosea:

God appeals to a backslidden nation to pray the prayer of repentance.

Joel:

Prayer in emergency: 1:19-20
Prayer and weeping: 2:17

Amos:

Prayer for respite and forgiveness: 7:1-9

Jonah:

Prayer of heathen sailors: 1:14-16
Prayer out of Hell: 2
Prayer of a repentant city: 3
Prayer of a displeased prophet: 4

Micah:

Prayer is waiting upon the Lord for fulfillment of His Word.

Habakkuk:

Prayer of complaint and vindication: 1:1-4,12-17
Prayer of faith: 3

Malachi:

Prayer - Protest one: 1:2
Prayer - Protest two: 1:6
Prayer - Protest three: 1:7,13
Prayer - Protest four: 2:17
Prayer - Protest five: 3:17
Prayer - Protest six: 3:8

PRAYERS IN THE NEW TESTAMENT

Matthew:

Prayer and the necessity of forgiveness: 5:22-26; 6:12,14-15
Prayer and hypocrisy: 6:5-7
Prayer as taught by Christ: 6:8-13
Prayer as specified by Christ: 7:7-11
Prayer of a leper: 8:1-4
Prayer of the centurion: 8:5-13
Prayer in peril: 8:23-27
Prayer of maniacs: 8:28-34
Prayer of Jairus: 9:18-19
Prayer of the diseased woman: 9:20-22
Prayer of two blind men: 9:27-31
Prayer of laborers: 9:37-39
Prayer of Christ's gratitude to God: 11:25-27
Prayer on a mountain: 14:23
Prayer of Peter in distress: 14:28-30
Prayer of Syro-Phoenician woman: 15:21-28
Prayer for a lunatic son: 17:14-21
Prayer in unity: 18:19-20
Prayer in a parable: 18:23-25
Prayer for a privileged position: 20:20-28
Prayer for healing of blindness: 20:29-34

Prayer of faith: 21:18-22
Prayer of pretense: 23:14,25
Prayer of accountability: 25:20,22,24
Prayer of a resigned will: 26:26,36-46
Prayer at Calvary: 27:46,50

Mark:

Prayer of a demon: 1:23-28,32-34
Prayer - Habits of Christ: 1:35; 6:41,46
Prayer for the deaf and dumb: 7:31-37
Prayer and fasting: 2:18; 9:29
Prayer of the young ruler: 10:17-22

Luke:

Prayer of Zacharias: 1:8,13,67-80
Prayer as a worship: 1:46-55
Prayer as adoration: 2:10-20,25-38
Prayer at the portal of service: 3:21-22
Prayer as escape from popularity: 5:16
Prayer and the twelve: 6:12-13,20,28
Prayer and transfiguration: 9:28-29
Prayer in parable form: 11:5-13
Prayer of the prodigal: 15:11-24,29-30
Prayer out of Hell: 16:22-31
Prayer of ten lepers: 17:12-19
Prayer in parable form: 18:1-8
Prayer of Pharisee and publican: 18:9-14
Prayer for Peter's preservation: 22:31-34
Prayer of agony: 22:39-46
Prayer and the risen Lord: 24:30,50-53

John:

Prayer for the spirit: 4:9,15,19,28; 7:37-39; 14:16
Prayer of a nobleman: 4:46-54
Prayer for the Bread of Life: 6:34
Prayer for Confirmation: 11:40-42
Prayer with a double aspect: 12:27-28
Prayer as a privilege: 14:13-15; 15:16; 16:23-26
Prayer of all prayers: 17

Acts:

Prayer in the upper chamber: 1:13-14
Prayer for a successor: 1:15-26
Prayer and worship: 2:42-47
Prayer as an observance: 3:1
Prayer for boldness of witness: 4:23-31
Prayer and the ministry of the Word: 6:4-7
Prayer of the first martyr: 7:55-60
Prayer for Samaritans and a sorcerer: 8:9-25
Prayer of a convert: 9:5-6,11
Prayer for Dorcas: 9:36-43
Prayer of Cornelius: 10:2-4,9,31
Prayer for Peter in prison: 12:5,12-17
Prayer of ordination: 13:2-3,43
Prayer with fasting: 13:2-3; 14:15,23,26
Prayer at the riverside: 16:13,16
Prayer in a dungeon: 16:25,34
Prayer of committal: 20:36
Prayer in a shipwreck: 27:33,35
Prayer for the fever-stricken: 28:8,15,28

Romans:

Prayer for a prosperous journey: 1:8-15
Prayer inspired by the Spirit: 8:15,23,26-27
Prayer for Israel's sake: 10:1; 11:26
Prayer as a continuing ministry: 12:12
Prayer for like-mindedness: 15:5-6,30-33
Prayer for Satan's conquest: 16:20,24-27

II Corinthians:

Prayer as a benediction: 1:2-4
Prayer for removal of thorn: 12:7-10

Ephesians:

Prayer and the believer's position: 1:1-11
Prayer for perception and power: 1:15-20
Prayer as access to God: 2:18; 3:12
Prayer for inner fullness: 3:13-21

Prayer and inner melody: 5:19-20
Prayer as a warrior's reserve: 6:18-19

Philippians:

Prayer as a request for joy: 1:2-7
Prayer and peace of mind: 4:6-7,19-23

Colossians:

Prayer as praise for loyalty: 1:1-8
Prayer for a seven-fold blessing: 1:9-14
Prayer fellowship: 4:2-4,12,17

I Thessalonians:

Prayer of remembrance: 1:1-3
Prayer for a return visit: 3:9-13
Prayer, praise and perfection: 5:17-18,23-24,28

II Thessalonians:

Prayer for worthiness of calling: 1:3,11-12
Prayer for comfort and stability: 2:13,16-17
Prayer for the Word and protection: 3:1-5

II Timothy:

Prayer for Timothy's ministry: 1:2-7
Prayer for the house of Onesiphorus: 1:6-18
Prayer for false friends: 4:14-18

Hebrews:

Prayer as praise for creation: 1:10-12
Prayer for mercy and favor: 4:16
Prayer and ministry of Christ: 5:7-8; 7:24-25
Prayer for the outworking of God's will: 12:9,12,15
Prayer for perfectness: 13:20-21

James:

Prayer for wisdom: 1:5-8,17
Prayer that misses the target: 4:2-3

Prayer that prevails: 5:13-18

I Peter:

Prayer of gratitude for inheritance: 1:3-4
Prayer in the married state: 3:7-12
Prayer-watch: 4:7
Prayer for Christian stability: 5:10-11

II Peter:

Prayer for multiplication of grace and peace: 1:2

III John:

Prayer the background of reputation: 1-4,12

Jude:

Prayer in the Spirit: 20

Revelation:

Prayer as praise to the Lamb for redemption: 5:9
Prayer as golden incense: 5:8; 8:3
Prayer of the martyred host: 6:10
Prayer of the Gentile host: 7:9-12
Prayer of the elders: 11:15-19
Prayer of Moses: 15:3-4
Prayer of the glorified saints: 19:1-10
Prayers ending the Bible: 22:17,20

(This prayer index is adapted from
"All The Prayers In The Bible"
by E.M. Bounds)

APPENDIX TWO
STUDY GUIDE: BIBLICAL INTERCESSION

Scriptural reference of the prayer:_______________________________________

Who prayed this prayer?_______________________________________

Biographical information on this person is given in the following references:

Positive spiritual qualities evident in the life of this intercessor:

List the qualities that made him/her a good intercessor. (These are things you want to emulate in your own life):

Negative qualities in this intercessor's life:

List qualities or conduct that interfered with their ministry of intercession.   (These are things you want to avoid in your own life):

Analysis of the prayer:

What events prompted the person to pray?
What is the main focus of the prayer?
What specific requests are made in the prayer?
What part of the prayer is intercession?   Petition? Confession? Worship and praise?
Is there evidence of faith or lack of faith by the person praying?
What Scriptures are quoted in the prayer?
What reference is made to God, Jesus, or the Holy Spirit?
List any promises of God claimed in the prayer.
Was the prayer answered?   When?   How?
If it wasn't answered, why not?
What were the results of the prayer?
What can you learn from this prayer to make your own intercession more effective?

ANSWERS TO SELF-TESTS

CHAPTER ONE:

1. Ask, and it shall be given you; seek, and ye shall find; knock, and it shall be opened unto you: For every one that asketh receiveth; and he that seeketh findeth, and to him that knocketh it shall be opened   (Matthew 7:7-8).

2. Prayer is communicating with God. It takes different forms, but basically it occurs when man talks with God and God talks with man.

3. The Bible reveals that prayer is answered:

Immediately at times:	Isaiah 65:24; Daniel 9:21-23
Delayed at times:	Luke 18:7
Different from our desires:	II Corinthians 12:8-9
Beyond our expectations:	Jeremiah 33:3; Ephesians 3:20

4. He made prayer a priority and it accompanied any event of importance in His life. See the section in Chapter One entitled "The Prayer Life Of Jesus."

5. There are three levels of intensity in prayer: Asking, seeking, and knocking: Asking is the first level of prayer. It is simply presenting a request to God and receiving an immediate answer.   Seeking is a deeper level of prayer. This is the level of prayer where answers are not as immediate as at the asking level. Knocking is a deeper level. It is prayer that is persistent when answers are longer in coming.

6. Worship and praise: Worship is the giving of honor and devotion. Praise is thanksgiving and an expression of gratitude not only for what God has done but for who He is. Commitment: This is prayer committing your life and will to God. It includes prayers of consecration and dedication to God, His work, and His purposes.   Petition: Petitions are requests made at the levels of asking, seeking, or knocking. Supplication is another word for this type of prayer. Confession and repentance: A prayer of confession is repenting and asking forgiveness for sin. Intercession: An intercessor is one who takes the place of another or pleads another's case.

CHAPTER TWO

1. Wherefore He is able also to save them to the uttermost that come unto God by Him, seeing He ever liveth to make intercession for them (Hebrews 7:25).

2. Intercession may be defined as holy, believing, persevering prayer whereby someone

pleads with God on behalf of another or others who desperately need God's intervention.

3.   The Biblical basis for the New Testament believer's ministry of intercessory prayer is our calling as priests unto God.   The Word of God declares that we are a holy priesthood (I Peter 2:5), a royal priesthood (I Peter 2:9), and a kingdom of priests (Revelation 1:5).

4.   Jesus Christ.

5.   As intercessors following the Old Testament priestly function and the New Testament pattern of Jesus, we stand before God and between a righteous God and sinful man.

6.   Intercession is important because of the emphasis Jesus placed on it in His own earthly ministry. Its importance is also revealed in the Biblical record which is filled with the stories of men and women who experienced powerful results through effective intercession. Through effective intercession, you can go spiritually anywhere in the world.

CHAPTER THREE:

1.   Then He called His twelve disciples together and gave them power and authority over all devils, and to cure diseases   (Luke 9:1).

2.   Your authority over the enemy comes through Jesus Christ and your position in Him as a believer. Your power over the enemy comes through the Holy Spirit.

3.   The term "to bind" originates from the Hebrew word *asar* meaning "to bind, imprison, tie, gird, to harness."   You can bind the power of the enemy to work in   your life, home, community, and church fellowship.

4.   To loose is to set free.   You can loose men and women from the bondage of sin, depression, and discouragement of the enemy.

5.   Matthew 16:19.

6.   The name of Jesus is powerful because it is the authority by which we intercede before God.   See John 14:14.

7.   Through the blood of Jesus we have access to God the Father.   Hebrews 10:19-22.

8.   The total fast is when you do not eat or drink at all. An example of this is found in Acts 9:9.   The partial fast is when the diet is restricted. An example of this is in Daniel 10:3.

9.   Fasting does not change God. It changes you. God relates to you on the basis of your relationship to Him.   When you change, then the way God deals with you is affected.

10.   Isaiah 58 describes God's "chosen" or divinely approved fast.

11.   When you fast, the first thing that happens is that God begins to reveal Himself to you (Isaiah 58:9). Other results of fasting itemized in Isaiah 58 are illumination, direction, provision, rejuvenation, and restoration.

CHAPTER FOUR:

1.   This is the confidence we have in approaching God; that if we ask anything according to His will, He hears us. And if we know that He hears us-whatever we ask-we know that we have what we asked of Him   (I John 5:14-15).

2.   Review the sections on how to intercede in Chapter Four.

3.   In Chapter Four, review the section on what we should intercede for in prayer.

4.   Review the principles for effective intercession in Chapter Four.

5.   You learn what God has promised and pray according to these promises, then you know your prayer will be answered. One way to do this is to go through the Bible and mark all the promises of God and then base your prayers upon these promises.

CHAPTER FIVE:

1.   Ye ask and receive not because ye ask amiss, that ye may consume it upon your lusts (James 4:3).

2.   Sin of any kind; idols in the heart; an unforgiving spirit; selfishness and wrong motives; wrong treatment of a marriage partner; self-righteousness; unbelief; not abiding in Christ and His Word; lack of compassion; hypocrisy, pride, meaningless repetition; not asking according to the will of God; not asking in Jesus' name; Satanic, demonic hindrances; not seeking first the kingdom; when you do not know how to pray as you should.

3.   When God has told you to do something. You should act upon the direction He has given and not use intercession as an excuse to avoid doing what God has commanded.

CHAPTER SIX:

1.   Our Father in heaven,
Hallowed be Your name.
Your kingdom come,
Your will be done.
On earth as it is in heaven.
Give us this day our daily bread.

And forgive us our debts,
As we forgive our debtors.
And do not lead us into temptation,
But deliver us from the evil one.
For Yours is the kingdom and the power and the glory forever.   Amen.
(Matthew 6:9-13)

2.   Matthew 6:9-13 and Luke 11:2-4.

3.   His prayer began with the plural possessive pronominal adjective "our."   Further in the prayer we see statements like "give us," "lead us," and "forgive us."   The model prayer is an intercessory prayer because you pray for others as well as yourself.

4.   Pray the prayer over them: "I pray that your Kingdom will come in her life, your will be done. Give her provision for this day..." etc.

5.   God's names represent His nature and what He is to us and you can claim this as you intercede for others.   For example, claim Jehovah-Jirah to provide for someone in need.

CHAPTER SEVEN:

1.   If my people, which are called by my name, shall humble themselves, and pray, and seek my face, and turn from their wicked ways; then will I hear from Heaven and will forgive their sin, and will heal their land (II Chronicles 7:14).

2.   A sovereign, extraordinary work of God through and in behalf of a people who   have learned and applied the principles revealed in the Rhemah Word of God regarding revival.

3.   We prepare for it by following the principles revealed in God's Word.   Revival is the joint move of the spirit of God and the response of the people of God.

4.   Revival is needed when   a backslidden condition is apparent.

5.   Compare your answer to the summary of evidences of a backslidden condition which are given in Chapter Seven.

6.   Compare your answer to the summary of Biblical principles of revival listed in Chapter Seven.

7.   Leadership, congregational, and general hindrances. See the discussion in Chapter Seven.

8.   II Chronicles 7:14.

9.   Humble yourself, pray, seek God's face, turn from your wicked ways.   See the discussion Chapter Seven.

CHAPTER EIGHT:

1.   But when you pray, go into your room, and when you have shut your door, pray to your Father who is in the secret place; and your Father who sees in secret will reward you openly   (Matthew 6:6).

2.   Answers will vary.

3.   Answers may include the following: Lack of time, distractions, tiredness, lack of desire.

4.   Answers will vary.

5.   Answers will vary.

6.   Answers will vary.